TRUTHS
THAT MAKE A
DIFFERENCE

The Doctrines Baptists Believe

Lavonn D. Brown

Revised Edition

Convention Press
Nashville, Tennessee

ISBN 0-8054-9594-0

This book is the text
for course number CG-0216 in the subject area
"Baptist Doctrine" of the Christian Growth Study Plan.

Dewey Decimal Classification Number: 230.6
Subject Headings: BAPTISTS-DOCTRINES

Printed in the United States of America
This book has been adapted from *I Believe* and *I Believe, Volume 2*.
Available from Baptist Book Stores

Unless indicated otherwise, all Scripture quotations are from the *New American Standard Bible.* Copyright © The Lockman Foundation, 1960, 1962, 1963, 1971, 1972, 1973, 1975, 1977. Used by permission. See *DiscipleYouth Bible,* Holman Bible Publishers, 1985.

Scripture quotations marked RSV are from the Revised Standard Version of the Bible, copyrighted 1946, 1952, © 1971, 1973.

Scripture quotations marked GNB are from the *Good News Bible,* the Bible in Today's English Version. Old Testament: Copyright © American Bible Society 1976; New Testament: Copyright © American Bible Society 1966, 1971, 1976. Used by permission.

Verses marked TLB are taken from *The Living Bible.* Copyright © Tyndale House Publishers, Wheaton, Illinois, 1971. Used by permission. Subsequent quotations are marked TLB.

Verses marked Phillips are reprinted with permission of Macmillan Publishing Co., Inc. from J. B. Phillips: *The New Testament in Modern English,* Revised Edition. © J. B. Phillips, 1958, 1960, 1972. Subsequent quotations are marked Phillips.

Verses marked KJV are taken from the King James Version of the Bible.

Verses marked NIV are from HOLY BIBLE *New International Version,* copyright © 1978, New York Bible Society. Used by permission. Subsequent quotations are marked NIV.

Youth Section
Discipleship and Family Development Division
The Sunday School Board of the Southern Baptist Convention
127 Ninth Avenue North
Nashville, TN 37234

Contents

The Writers

Lavonn D. Brown, writer of the content material in this book, is pastor of First Baptist Church, Norman, Oklahoma. A well-known Southern Baptist pastor, speaker, and leader, he has served as president of the Oklahoma Baptist Convention. He and his wife, Norma Lee, a talented artist, are the parents of three sons—Bob, Scott, and Nathan.

To form the framework of this book, Dr. Brown used questions youth asked about basic Baptist doctrines. Printed first as *I Believe* and *I Believe, Volume 2,* this book gives unity to a doctrinal study of major Baptist beliefs.

Karen Dockrey, writer of the personal learning activities (Truth-Search) and the Group Learning Activities, is a free-lance writer and homemaker. Author of *Getting to Know God,* she has written for a number of Southern Baptist publications.

A longtime worker with youth, Karen currently is a youth leader at Bluegrass Baptist Church, Hendersonville, Tennessee. She and her husband, Bill, are the parents of two daughters: Emily and Sarah.

Introduction

I remember one youth asking, "Who 'makes up' the Baptist beliefs?" Any answer must begin, *"No one person."* In this respect, Baptists are an amazing people. No one person would ever attempt to write an official statement of Baptist beliefs. The materials projected in this book are the efforts of one Southern Baptist. The 1963 statement of *The Baptist Faith and Message* is the doctrinal guideline. It is hoped that the final product will be in agreement with the faith and message of Baptists everywhere.

These materials are presented with a prayer that people will be helped and encouraged in their search for truth. Some people may feel that they are overexposed to truth. Nevertheless, truth should never be feared. Nor should it be rejected as truth merely because of its source.

Are you ready for the search into *truths that make a difference?* If so, begin with a Bible nearby. Pray for the guidance of the Holy Spirit as you seek to discover God's truths. And, remember, it is possible to affirm some truths while we search for deeper understanding of other truths.

1

What Is God Like?

Memory Verses: *John 4:24; 1 John 1:5; 1 John 4:8* (cards 1-3)

Let's begin our search for truth with a study of the nature of

θεός
God

The symbol of our search will be a circle for infinity— ( )
without beginning, without end.

Putting our faith into words is never easy. And, even after we do, we receive new insights. Our faith is never a final faith. We cannot store it for safekeeping.

> ■■ So, let me affirm one of the basic elements of my faith: I BELIEVE IN GOD. For me, this is a *truth that makes a difference.* I do not understand everything there is to know about God, but that does not disturb me. This is a confession of faith that I must make.
>
> **Remember,** it is possible to affirm our belief in God while we continue our search for greater understanding.

You believe in God? Good for you! But what does that mean? The important question to answer is, What kind of God do you believe in? Do you believe that human beings have been created in the image of God or that God has been created in the image of human beings? Do you believe that God's nature is such that He created people for fellowship or that the human nature is such that people "designed" God for their own comfort?

TruthSearch 1

At this moment, what is God like to you? Use words, symbols, shapes, or drawings to express your ideas about God.

During the last two months as I have been through the storms of life. I have identified God as my life Savior. He is my Savior and he gives me life. John 3:16. As I prayer without stopping he gives me the desires of my heart. He's my life Savior. My true friend who I lean and depend and remain to trust and believe

What God Is Not Like

J. B. Phillips wrote a book entitled _Your God Is Too Small_. In this book he expressed his feeling that many people live with inner dissatisfaction or without any faith simply because their concept of God makes Him too small.

Often, people get trapped by an inadequate concept of God. Some are like the schoolboy who was asked what he thought God was like. He

answered, "The sort of person who is always snooping around to see if anyone is having a good time and trying to stop it." For this boy, God is much like the "Resident Policeman" concept suggested by J. B. Phillips. In such a case it is difficult to tell the difference between God and the voice of human conscience. God becomes a cosmic killjoy who finds great pleasure in keeping people from having a good time. Is this your concept of God? If so, you have an unsatisfactory view of what God is like.

Many psychologists propose that our early concept of God is closely related to our idea of father. Phillips has called this a "parental hangover." Perhaps this view is a natural stage in the process of a maturing faith. A concept of God that is based primarily on fear, however, will never provide a satisfactory foundation for mature Christianity.

Some people view God as a "Grand Old Man," who "was a great power in His day, but could not possibly be expected to keep pace with modern progress!"[1] To such people, God is an old gentleman with a long beard and gray hair. He sits on a great, ornate throne "up there" gazing down at the world of people. This concept of God as old (and consequently old-fashioned) is inadequate.

A further view of God pictures Him as a magnified human being—a giant man. With this view of God He becomes a "Managing Director," responsible for the successful operation of a vast universe. He cannot be expected to take detailed interest in a single human life. When we think of God in such human terms, He becomes little more than a frustrated telephone operator sitting at a giant switchboard, busily plugging in on poor mortals. Remember, human beings are made in the image of God and not God made in the image of human beings.

I am not implying that the concepts of God just described are false. The point is that they are inadequate and incomplete. In some of these instances God is "too small." In others, God is "too big."

Will the Real God Please Stand Up?

Is it possible for us to know the real God? Yes, it is possible. But most of us have to work our way around some inadequate concepts in coming to know the real God. That's no problem, as long as we do not get discouraged and quit trying.

How is it possible to know the real God? God has made Himself known in many ways. He speaks through many voices. He has left us with many sources of knowledge concerning Himself. When Paul and Barnabas attempted to tell the Gentiles at Lystra about the living God, they said, "He has always given evidence of his existence by the good things he does: he gives you rain from heaven and crops at the right times; he gives you food and fills your hearts with happiness" (Acts 14:17, GNB).

TruthSearch 2

Write or draw a way each of the following persons and things can teach us about God. After reading the personal testimony in the following paragraphs, you may want to add to each category.

CHRISTIANS
Testimonies
Love /comfort

NATURE
The existance
The sounds
The ongoing

THE BIBLE
The men begin inspired by God

JESUS
His existance
Birth, death, burial
resurrection, promise ascention
The teaching
Just
evangelical
Salvation
United
Savior

As I think back over my own experience, I discover that God made Himself known to me in various ways. God kept breaking into my world of awareness even though my home would probably fall in the category of "nominally Christian." If you would permit me a personal testimony, I would like to tell you how I came to believe in God or how God revealed Himself to me.

1. *God made Himself known to me in His people.* My earliest impressions of God came by observation. My mother was a praying and compassionate woman. My father, though not a Christian at the time, made it possible for me to believe in a God who loves, cares, and provides for His own. My heritage was enriched by devout, churchgoing grandparents. Christian homes, churchgoing youth, worn Bibles, churches, and Chrisitan art all spoke to me of God.

God had His "living letters," and I read every one of them. These were human letters "written not with ink, but with the Spirit of the living God, not on tablets of stone, but on tablets of human hearts" (2 Cor. 3:3). Some of these letters were confusing to me, as I know they must be to you. Others were unmistakably clear. These bothered me. They reminded me of a God I was trying to forget.

I watched God at work in His people, producing the fruits of the Spirit—gentleness, kindness, and thoughtfulness. In fact, God was producing in them those virtues that were noticeably absent in my own life. I was never able to discard what God was so obviously accomplishing in the lives of His people.

When all other evidence failed, there remained one evidence that was impossible to ignore: the changes God brought about in human nature.

2. *Next, God made Himself known in His creation.* For me, God became increasingly necessary to explain an ordered universe and the human moral consciousness.

God began to speak a new language. When I looked into the microscope and telescope, God spoke the language of beauty, order, harmony, balance, design, and predictability. The heavens began telling of the glory of God. The earth was "declaring the work of His hands" (Ps. 19:1).

The "image of God" in human beings was never difficult for me to accept or believe. A person's ability to begin, achieve, do, and finish all revealed the divine imprint. I was never able to accept casually human intelligence, sense of right and wrong, and universal awareness of divine presence. All these spoke to me of God.

I realize that neither design in nature nor human moral capacity can prove God to one who chooses not to believe. Even though these experiences were not conclusive, they were powerful. I could not ignore them altogether.

3. *Then, God made Himself known to me through the Bible—His written Word.* When I was in high school, for reasons unknown to me, I began reading the Bible. I discovered an old, half-burned Bible in the projection room of the local theatre where I worked. During the brief intervals between the reels of film, I read the Bible. As I read the thrilling stories, it slowly dawned on me that these were real people in a real world who had undergone real experiences with a real God.

God began to speak a new language. His approach at this time was more direct, more personal. At the same time, there seemed to be a maturing in my own receptiveness to God's attempt to reveal Himself.

The Scriptures began to have a "ring of truth" about them. There was something within me that reached out in highest hope toward the One beginning to reveal Himself. The Bible took on the characteristics of authority, sufficiency, and certainty, even though no one had told me that "All Scripture is inspired by God" (2 Tim. 3:16).

I discovered that the Bible called for a life-style and a type of moral character that would be more acceptable to God. I fell far short of the expected quality of life. In fact, I doubted if I would even register on the quality scales. If someone had asked me, "Do you understand what you are reading?" my answer would have been, "How can I unless someone helps me?" At this point no one had told me, "These have been written in order that you may believe that Jesus is the Messiah, the Son of God, and that through your faith in Him you may have life" (John 20:31, GNB).

4. *Finally, God made himself known to me in His Son—Jesus Christ.* I do not know exactly when the awareness came. As I read the life of Christ in the Gospels, I slowly began to realize that in Him we see what God must be like.

What is God like? The early disciples looked at Jesus and saw something eternally true about God. Paul wrote: "God was in Christ reconciling the world to Himself" (2 Cor. 5:19). After showing that God had spoken in many different ways through the ages, the writer of Hebrews concluded, "In these last days he has spoken to us through his Son" (Heb. 1:2, GNB). John wrote, "No one has ever seen God. The only Son, . . . has made him known" (John 1:18, GNB).

God clearly made Himself known to me. At the time, I could have given you many reasons why I did not want to become a Christian. But God kept breaking into my world. I could no longer plead ignorance of Him—only indifference.

I knew I could not go on ignoring God indefinitely. I realized that the life I was living would not do. So, I listened with new ears to His soft, but insistent, voice as He spoke to me concerning the emptiness and meaninglessness of my life. He promised that a new life was awaiting me. I searched. I believed. I followed. Only then did the Holy Spirit move in with the assurance, certainty, and presence of God that I so desired.

God Is Spirit

Three statements in the New Testament help us understand what God is like: "God is spirit" (John 4:24); "God is light" (1 John 1:5); and "God is love" (1 John 4:8). While these three statements affirm some things about

God that are eternally true, they also rule out many false concepts about Him.

TruthSearch 3

Unscramble the words to quote each memory verse:

John 4:24   and and is in spirit, spirit God those who worship worship Him must truth

God is Spirit, and those who worship him, must worship him in Spirit and truth

1 John 1:5   And at all this in is is is the message we have from Him Him and and to you, that God light, heard announce darkness there no

This is the message which we have heard from Him and declare to you, that God is light and in Him is no darkness at all.

1 John 4:8   know is The one who does not not love love does God God, for

The one who does not love does not know God, for God is love

Jesus declared that "God is spirit" (John 4:24). The witness to God as spirit is found in the first chapter of the Bible: "The Spirit of God was moving over the surface of the waters" (Gen. 1:2). And the last chapter of the Bible also affirms God as spirit: "The Spirit and the bride say, 'Come.'" (Rev. 22:17). All in between is God's revelation and humankind's discovery of God as spirit.

Before this affirmation can be fully understood, we need to carefully investigate the occasion for Jesus' statement. He made the statement at a time when He felt that He "had to" go through Samaria. Why did He feel this moral necessity? His disciples would have discouraged His going into Samaritan territory. After all, the Jews avoided any contact with the Samaritans. Even though it was closer to go through Samaria on the way from Judea to Galilee, the Jews took another route because of their hatred for the Samaritans. Rather than go through Samaria, they crossed the Jordan and traveled on the eastern side of the river through Perea on to Galilee. So, why did Jesus decide to go through Samaria? Let's see.

About noon, Jesus and His group arrived at the small village of Sychar in Samaria and went to Jacob's well. The long walk and hot sun had taken their toll. Jesus was tired. He sat down at the well to rest. The disciples went to the market area in Sychar to buy food.

While Jesus sat alone at the well, a woman came to draw water. We learn later that she had a bad reputation because of her questionable life-style. Jesus knew all about her way of living. It is always a surprise—though it shouldn't be—to discover that Jesus spoke some of His most remarkable words to the least remarkable people.

For a starter, Jesus asked the woman for a drink of water. The woman's response was typical, influenced by many years of prejudice. "'How is it that you, being a Jew, ask me for a drink since I am a Samaritan woman?' (For Jews have no dealings with Samaritans.)"

Jesus understood the woman's feelings and responded with a gentle reminder, "'If you only knew what God gives and who it is that is asking you for a drink, you would ask him, and he would give you life-giving water'" (John 4:10, GNB). Jesus proceeded to tell her about the water that did not come from Jacob's well—water that would become an ever-flowing stream within, springing up into eternal life.

In the course of the conversation, the words of Jesus began to get too close to home. He started talking about the woman's life-style. She tried to change the subject by asking for Jesus' opinion about the best place to worship—in Jerusalem or at Mount Gerizim.

Jesus' remarkable answer contained the affirmation, "God is Spirit." He replied, "God is spirit, and those who worship Him must worship in spirit and truth" (John 4:24).

What do you think Jesus was trying to tell us about God when He said, "God is spirit"? Right now take a minute to write down what "God is spirit" means to you.

He is Sovereign, Supreme, Super,
He is their. He is almighty
He is Sad.

God is Spirit, and those who worship Him must worship in spirit and truth.

Before we look further at the meaning of "God is spirit," perhaps it would be good to note what is ruled out by this important concept. If God is spirit, then some of our false and inadequate concepts of God are ruled out. For instance, many people appear to worship a God who was created in the image of a human being. If God is spirit, we must rule out the idea that God is simply a projection of our childish desire for a loving, Heavenly Father. We also must rule out the idea that God has a body with feet, arms, hands, eyes, ears, and a mouth like a human being. If God is spirit, we must eliminate the idea that God has to think as we think, have the same human characteristics we have, and automatically hold the same opinions we have. We must confess that His ways are above our ways, and His thoughts are above our thoughts.

Some people consider religious faith as a form of psychological "escapism." They feel that those who place faith in God are attempting to escape from the realities of life. If God is spirit, however, we must rule out the concept that God is "a heavenly hideaway" out there somewhere to which people fly to escape.

Now, let's consider what is affirmed by this concept. If God is spirit . . . then what? What does this tell us about the nature of God, and what we can expect from Him?

In the first place, we know that *God is invisible.* He cannot be seen by the human eye. John asserted, "No one has ever seen God" (John 1:18, GNB). The Colossian letter speaks of the invisible or unseen God (see Col. 1:15). This idea seems simple enough. Yet, it is one of the most difficult ideas for us to accept. The history of worshiping idols is the history of people attempting to make God visible. People have tried to assign form, location, space, and time to God. This problem is in the background of the First Commandment: "'Worship no god but me. Do not make for yourselves images of anything. . . . for I am the Lord your God'" (Deut. 5:7-9, GNB).

The second truth related to God as spirit is that *He is present everywhere.* Therefore, He can be worshiped anywhere. Jesus told the Samaritan woman about a time when people will not worship God on Mount Gerizim or in Jerusalem (John 4:21). God is not confined to a certain place. He is not restricted by time and space. He cannot be confined to mountaintops nor enclosed by church walls (see Ps. 139:7-12).

Because God is spirit and, therefore, present everywhere, we may affirm a third great truth: *God is always near and approachable.* He is personally present with every believer. John stated: "No one has ever seen God, but if we love one another, God lives in union with us, and his love is made perfect in us" (1 John 4:12, GNB).

Because God is spirit, we must be genuine and sincere in our worship.

Jesus said that we must worship Him in spirit and in truth. This would be the very opposite of pretense and shallowness. We must think that God is naive if we imagine that He does not see through our pretense, shallowness, and unworthy motives.

God Is Light

"God is light" (1 John 1:5) is a second great affirmation that tells what God is like. Just as the truth that God is spirit is evident in the first chapter of the Bible, God as light is also apparent in that chapter: "Then God said, 'Let there be light'; and there was light. And God saw that the light was good; and God separated the light from the darkness" (Gen. 1:3-4). And, in the last chapter of the Bible we read, "There shall no longer be any night; and they shall not have need of the light of a lamp nor the light of the sun, because the Lord God shall illumine them; and they shall reign forever and ever" (Rev. 22:5). In between these chapters, there runs a continual contrast between light and darkness.

People speak a universal language that says we love light and fear darkness. Light stands for life, truth, reality, holiness, and glory. Darkness stands for ignorance, sin, nothingness, moral blindness, and death. It is little wonder that John affirmed, "God is light." Physically, light represents glory; intellectually, it represents truth; morally, it represents holiness.

This insight into God's nature was not exactly new with John. The Old Testament contains many references to God as light. The psalmist declared, "The Lord is my light and my salvation; Whom shall I fear?" (Ps. 27:1). The prophet, Isaiah, wrote, "You will have the Lord for an everlasting light, And your God for your glory" (Isa. 60:19). The theme of light became a key to understanding prophecy about the Messiah: "The people who walk in darkness Will see a great Light; Those who live in a dark land, The light will shine on them." (Isa. 9:2).

The New Testament references to light and darkness are less frequent but have fuller meaning. In the beginning verses of John's Gospel, he made it clear that the light Jesus brings will overcome the world's darkness. "Eternal life is in him, and this life gives light to all mankind. His life is the light that shines through the darkness—and the darkness can never extinguish it" (John 1:4-5, TLB). The light Jesus brings to humanity has an unconquerable quality. When His light comes, darkness is dispelled, but His light is not defiled. The light of Christ puts to flight man's oldest fear—the fear of darkness.

The light that Christ brings shows things exactly as they are. His light strips away disguises and masks. In the beginning of His public ministry, Jesus said to Nicodemus: "The light is come into the world, and men loved the darkness rather than the light; for their deeds were evil. For everyone who does evil hates the light, and does not come to the light, lest his deeds should be exposed" (John 3:19-20). Paul said, "For light is capable of 'showing up' everything for what it really is" (Eph. 5:13, Phillips). At times this is the last thing most of us would want to happen.

On two different occasions Jesus declared, "I am the light of the world" (John 8:12; 9:5). This is a claim Jesus made concerning Himself; therefore, it gives us insight into the nature and character of God. The first occasion for His declaration was during the Feast of Tabernacles. On the first evening of this annual festival, the people gathered in one of the courts of the Temple for the ceremony of lighting four golden candlesticks. When the four great candelabra were glowing, their light extended throughout Jerusalem. With this background Jesus said: "I am the light of the world; he who follows Me shall not walk in the darkness, but shall have the light of life" (John 8:12). The second occasion for Jesus' statement was after He had restored the sight of the man born blind (see John 9:5).

The light of Christ is intended to eliminate the world's darkness. The followers of Christ have a responsibility to help this happen as they become reflectors of that light: "You are the world's light . . . glowing in the night for all to see. . . . Let it shine for all" (Matt. 5:14-15, TLB). Just as the moon, dark in itself, reflects the light of the sun, each follower of Christ is to reflect His heavenly light into the world's darkness.

When John affirmed that "God is light, and in Him there is no darkness at all" (1 John 1:5), he was trying to help us become better acquainted with the real God. What does this great affirmation tell us about God? First of all, it tells us that God wishes to be known. Light is self-revealing. There is nothing secretive or concealed about God. Second, the affirmation speaks of the purity and holiness of God. Light is the complete opposite of everything evil and dark. For that reason, the light of the gospel makes persons aware of sin in their lives. The light calls for open honesty with God at the point of the basic wrongness, purposelessness, and meaninglessness of our lives. Finally, the concept of God as light speaks of God's interest in guiding our lives. His light makes our path clear. Our future paths are gradually illuminated as His light shines "more and more." His word becomes a lamp to our feet and a light to our paths. Our responsibility is to walk in that light.

God Is Love

What is God like? "God is love" (1 John 4:8). This affirmation is part of the most beautiful and profound passage in John's letter.

TruthSearch 4

Read 1 John 4:17-21. After reading the passage, complete the following sentences:

God showed His love for me by

Because God loves me, I ought to

Abiding in God makes me feel

There is no fear in true love because

You can tell if someone loves God by the way he or she treats

First John 4:7-21 is an outstanding contribution to our understanding of both divine and human love. Perhaps the following diagram will give you a summary of love relationships explored by John.

God is the source of love: "Love is from God" (1 John 4:7).

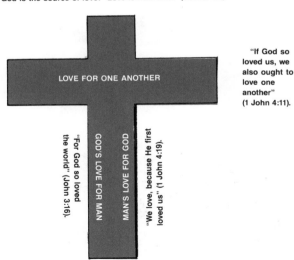

LOVE FOR ONE ANOTHER

"If God so loved us, we also ought to love one another" (1 John 4:11).

GOD'S LOVE FOR MAN

"For God so loved the world" (John 3:16).

MAN'S LOVE FOR GOD

"We love, because He first loved us" (1 John 4:19).

John was careful to point out that God is the source of love (1 John 4:7). Our ability to love is merely a reflection of divine love. When we love as God loves we are expressing what we were meant to be and do.

As the source of love, God actively expresses love for people. He has expressed His love so much that John felt love was the most accurate description of what God is like: "God is love." When you consider God's attributes, you will discover that love is closely related to all of them.

Is it too much to hope that God's love is constant? Many people are exposed to a kind of love that is conditional. Love is shown only when certain conditions are met. "Do this; don't do that; and I will love you." When these conditions are not met, love is withdrawn. God's love is not optional or conditional; it is constant.

Actually, it is by love that God is best known and most often discovered. We see the results of His love at work in the lives of His people. No one has ever seen the wind; only the effect of the wind is seen. No one has ever seen God; only the effect of His love is seen.

Maybe you have questions, such as:

- If God is a God of love, why is the world in the mess it is in?
- How can God love someone like me?
- Why does God allow evil?
- Does God *really* have a plan for *my* particular life?
- Is it possible that I can be someone of worth in God's eyes and in the eyes of others?

TruthSearch 5

Choose the question from the list just given that troubles you the most. Write a possible answer to it. (HINT: Don't feel bad if you struggle with these questions—other believers have been puzzled by them throughout the centuries!)

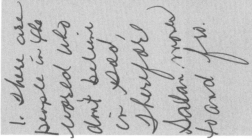

The questions asked above find their partial answer, at least, in the fact that God is love. He created us with the freedom to make our own choices, because He wanted our love to be free and spontaneous. Otherwise, He would have made us robots or puppets. In the commentary, *The Gospel of John,* by William Barclay we are reminded that love is not love unless a person is free not to love. God went to the trouble to redeem us, because a God of love must seek and save the lost. He gives us eternal life, because a God of love desires to have continual, eternal fellowship with persons created in His image.

The greatest demonstration of God's love is found in the gift of His Son: "God showed his love for us by sending his only Son into the world, so that we might have life through him. This is what love is" (1 John 4:9-10, GNB). Without the life, love, and death of Christ, John could never have said, "God is love." If you want to understand the meaning of the statement *God is love,* then study the life of Christ, keeping in mind that He said, "'He who has seen Me has seen the Father'" (John 14:9).

Because God is love, we have the ability to love. We are created in the image of a God of love. Human love is a response to revealed divine love. And it is expected that this human love will be expressed to others. It should be expressed in two directions: in love for God and in love for others.

God loved first, and our love for Him and others is expressed in response to His love (see 1 John 4:19). Our ability to love is not merely the product of human love; it is a gift from God.

In John's mind, love for God and love for others were inseparable (read 1 John 4:11). The only way to prove our love for God is to love the people God loves. John pointed out how difficult it is to separate love for God and love for others: "If someone says he loves God, but hates his brother, he is a liar. For he cannot love God, whom he has not seen, if he does not love his brother, whom he has seen" (1 John 4:20, GNB).

An American journalist in China watched a missionary nurse cleaning the sores of wounded soldiers in a hospital. "I wouldn't do that for a million dollars," the visitor said.

Without pausing in her work, the nurse quietly replied, "Neither would I." And such is love, a gift from God.

As emphasized at the beginning of this chapter, it is possible to affirm some things while we continue the search for greater understanding. It is my firm conviction that no one has been left completely alone by God. My prayer is that you can now affirm, "I BELIEVE IN GOD."

Are you actively seeking God? If not, why not? Could it be that you fear the changes He would want to make in your life? In the book *Mere Christianity,* C. S. Lewis told what he often did as a child when a toothache developed. He knew if he went to his mother, she would give him something to deaden the pain and make it possible for him to sleep. He also knew something else. She would take him to the dentist the next morning. The dentist would not be content just to relieve the pain. He would want to set all his teeth permanently right. So, the boy determined to bear the pain as long as possible.

Many people avoid going to God for the same reason. They would like to be cured of the particular sin, but they know God would not stop there. Once you call Him in, He will give you the full treatment. If He is spirit, light, and love, however, you could be in no safer, more sympathetic hands.

Honestly Now

Write a letter to God. This letter is not to be shared with anyone. Name the three most important things in your life. Tell God how much you need His love and how you love Him. End your letter with this thought: "I am a person of worth because I have been created in the image of God. God is love."

---

[1]J. B. Phillips, *Your God Is Too Small* (New York: The Macmillan Company, 1961). vi. Used by permission.

2

When God Became Flesh

Memory Verses: *Matthew 16:16; John 1:14* (cards 4-5)

The next area of our search for truth will involve us in a study of the nature of

χριστός
Christ

The symbol of our search will be the fish— one of the early symbols for Christianity.

The reason for selecting this symbol is simple. The Greek word for fish formed an acrostic with special meaning:

$$
\begin{array}{rcl}
\text{I} &=& \text{Jesus} \\
\text{X} &=& \text{Christ} \\
\theta &=& \text{God} \\
\gamma &=& \text{Son} \\
\Sigma &=& \text{Savior}
\end{array}
$$

In each part of the acrostic the Greek letter listed is the first letter in the Greek word for the name. Altogether the acrostic reads, "Jesus Christ, God, Son, Savior." Early followers of Christ, under constant threat of persecution, used the sign of the fish to let others know they were Christians.

In the previous chapter we stated that God has made Himself known in many ways and through many witnesses. The most personal and unmistakable revelation of God was in His Son—Jesus Christ.

■■ I BELIEVE IN CHRIST. I also believe that, in Jesus Christ, God has come to humanity. This is a *truth that has made a difference* in my life. I do not understand everything there is to know about the divine-human Christ. Yet, I am not disturbed. It is a confession of faith that I must make.

Remember, it is possible to affirm our belief in Christ while we continue our search for greater understanding of "God in the flesh."

So you believe in Christ? Tremendous! The question is, Who is Jesus Christ? The answer to that question will determine whether this is a truth that makes a difference in your life.

TruthSearch 6

If you had to describe Jesus Christ to someone who had never heard of Him, what would you say? Write your description.

Inadequate Concepts of Christ

Many people live with totally inadequate concepts of Christ. Their indifference to Christ is the only evidence needed to prove this point. No one can come to a knowledge of Christ as Son of God and remain indifferent.

"I feel that Jesus was a great man," said one young person. "He had great insight and empathy, but he was just a great prophet, not the son of God." Most people are willing to add the name of Jesus to their long list of the greatest men who ever lived. Yes, Christians and many non-Christians agree that Christ was the greatest man who ever lived. But is that all we can say?

Many non-Christians look upon Jesus as a great human teacher. They are deeply impressed by His wisdom and insight. Even people of other religions praise Him for His high moral values. Some people admire Him because He heads their list as the Master Teacher. But is that the final truth? Can nothing more be said?

The place was Caesarea Philippi in the Holy Land. For the disciples of Jesus, it was exam day. People had many opinions about His identity. Jesus needed a clear-cut confession from His followers as to who they thought He was.

Hostility toward Jesus was growing. Jesus had sought an opportunity to be alone with His disciples. He knew the end was near. Had anyone recognized Him for who and what He was? Would there be anyone to carry on His work? The survival of His mission was at stake.

Jesus began His challenge with an easy question, "Who do people say that the Son of Man is?" (See Matt. 16:13.)

The disciples felt they could answer this question, because popular opinions were numerous.

Peter, as spokesman for the group, replied, "Some say John the Baptist; and others, Elijah; but still others, Jeremiah, or one of the prophets" (Matt. 16:14).

People generally believed that Jesus was someone great. He was considered the reincarnation of one of the greatest prophets. Surely Jesus would be satisfied to be classified in such great company.

The wise Examiner moved gently from the simple to the difficult, from the impersonal to the personal. He asked them, "Who do *you* say that I am?" (Matt. 16:15). This was the question of all questions, and the answer did not come easily. But Simon Peter did not disappoint his Lord. Are you ready for his answer?

"Thou art the Christ, the Son of the living God" (Matt. 16:16).

Essentially, Peter had discovered that no human categories, descriptions, or classifications were adequate to describe Jesus Christ. Jesus

was more than a great man, teacher, or prophet. This conviction came by living in the company and presence of Jesus. After Peter's great and noble confession, Jesus knew His work was in safe hands.

Will the Real Jesus Please Stand Up?

Almost two thousand years ago, in Galilee, there lived a man who knew God. His name was Jesus. He came to be known as the Christ—the Anointed One. His name is familiar to nearly everyone. But is it possible to know His name while the man Himself remains a mystery?

A number of years ago I knew a lovely young girl named Norma Lee. At first I was content to know her name. As we became better acquainted, I was more interested in knowing the person behind the name. Our relationship matured to the point that I asked her to marry me. After more than twenty years of marriage, the name is still precious. Over the years, I have come to love, appreciate, and respond to the person behind the name. Many people know her by name. I know her as a person of worth who brings out the best in me.

It is possible for individuals to grow up in a Christian home, faithfully attend a Christian church, study the Bible in Sunday School, and still know little about Jesus Christ as a person. Coming to know a person requires a commitment similar to marriage. In that continuing commitment we come to love, appreciate, and respond to the person who bears the name.

The real Jesus is worth knowing. In Jesus, God has come to us. At one definite point, the living God broke through into history.

Our family loves to spend some time each summer in the Colorado mountains. I always enjoy coming to a high mountain pass where the water courses divide and flow in separate directions. Even though I have seen it many times, the wonder remains. Raindrops falling on one side of the Continental Divide flow eastward and ultimately wind their way toward the Atlantic. Only a few yards away raindrops form a tiny stream to begin a long winding journey westward toward the Pacific. I experience a reverence to know I am standing at the watershed, where all the streams divide.

Jesus Christ has split history in much the same way. Every event in human history is now dated with reference to His coming. History is divided into two eras—BC (before Christ) and AD (*anno Domini*, Latin for "In the Year of Our Lord"). Any person who has so influenced human history is worth knowing.

TruthSearch 7

Fill in the blanks to state reasons Jesus is worth knowing:

1. Jesus is the Christ which means the _____ One.

2. At a definite point, the living _____ broke through into history. In Jesus, God _____ to us.

3. Jesus has divided _____.

Then God Became Flesh

God made human beings in His image. He took a calculated risk when He made people free. God desired to love and be loved. He made us with free will and choice, because He wanted our love to be free and spontaneous.

In exercising their free will, man and woman chose the way of sin and rebellion. The results: Human beings were separated from the God of love, severed from their own better self, and isolated from perfect fellowship with other people.

God was faced with a challenging problem. On one hand were sinful people living in deliberate rebellion. On the other hand was a holy God who must be both loving and just. How could the holy God and the sinful people be brought together? God could not condemn all humanity because that would be inconsistent with love. He could not save all humanity indiscriminately because that would be inconsistent with justice.

One other alternative or choice was open to God. He could send a mediator who would pay the price He Himself demanded, leaving the decision with people of free will. John described this alternative when he said, "Before anything else existed, there was Christ, [the Word] with God. He has always been alive and is himself God. . . . And Christ became a human being and lived here on earth among us and was full of loving forgiveness and truth" (John 1:1,14, TLB). At one point in history God became flesh and lived among people.

We call God's carefully chosen alternative the *incarnation*. The name is derived from the Latin words *in carnis* meaning "in the flesh." What the incarnation actually affirms is that the man Jesus of Nazareth was in a unique sense the self-expression of God.

The word *incarnation* does not appear in the Bible, but the concept does: "For in the Christ there is all of God in a human body" (Col. 2:9,

TLB). Paul also wrote, "For God was in Christ, restoring the world to himself" (2 Cor. 5:19, TLB). In the incarnation we are confronted with a great miracle: God revealed Himself in a flesh and blood body. We are also confronted with a great mystery that is beyond human understanding. The doctrine of the incarnation is an expression of the Christian conviction that Jesus was truly man and, at the same time, truly God.

TruthSearch 8

Define *incarnation* by writing a word or phrase that begins with or contains each letter. Use the material in this section, your Bible, and your own insight. An example has been completed:

God **In** a human body

N

C

A

R

N

A

T

I

O

N

Was Jesus Fully Human?

Christians have always had difficulty realizing that Jesus was fully, completely, and truly human. It is easier to think of Him as God in human disguise. For two thousand years people have occasionally claimed that Jesus was a divine being who merely *seemed* to be human.

Read the Gospel accounts again. The dominant fact that stands out in these writings is that Jesus was a man—an extraordinary man, to be sure, but nonetheless a man. Three facts about Jesus point to His humanity.

1. Jesus' birth was a *human birth*. We often lose sight of the humanity of Jesus' birth because of the star, the angelic announcements, the heavenly choirs, and the Wise Men. It is difficult to concentrate on the human aspects when we read about the sky being punctured by voices and heaven coming down to earth. But let's try.

Mary was a human mother. She should be neither worshiped nor ignored. Scholars and historians insist that she was a young woman. Because she shared the fallen nature common to all humanity, Mary was a sinner.

We have reason to believe that Mary was a happy woman. She was happy because she was betrothed. Betrothal was more than engagement. It was a solemn agreement that could be broken only by a bill of divorcement. She was happy because she was in love with Joseph, the village carpenter. She loved him, not because he was rich or handsome, but because she knew he was a good, kind, devoted, gentle man. She was also a woman of unusual faith. When the angel told Mary that she had been chosen of God to be the mother of Jesus, the Son of God, she responded, "'I am the Lord's servant, and I am willing to do whatever he wants. May everything you said come true'" (Luke 1:38, TLB).

This situation left Joseph with a human problem. After the angel's announcement, Mary hurried to the highlands of Judea to visit her cousin Elizabeth. When she returned to her hometown about three months later, Mary was found to be pregnant. Joseph's reaction probably followed normal human patterns—from cold unbelief to open rage, and finally, to stunned amazement. Two choices were open to him. He could either expose Mary before the court or divorce her privately. Love caused him to decide on the latter.

If ever a man needed a word from God, Joseph did. The word came. One night as Joseph lay considering all that had happened, an angel spoke to him. "'Joseph, son of David, . . don't hesitate to take Mary as your wife! For the child within her has been conceived by the Holy Spirit'" (Matt. 1:20, TLB). Joseph was also a person of great faith. When he awoke, "He did as the angel commanded, and brought Mary home to be his wife" (Matt. 1:24, TLB).

Near the time for Jesus' birth, Mary decided to make an eighty-mile trip to Bethlehem. She did not want to be away from Joseph when her child was born. A bedlam of noise filled their ears as they made their way to the village inn, already crowded to overflowing. Joseph bedded his wife down in the area provided for animals. The place for Jesus' birth was a stable. No physician stood by. Only the calloused hands of a carpenter— hands made tender by love—came to her aid. The crib was a manger— feeding trough for animals. With unsurpassed beauty and amazing re-

straint Luke recorded that Mary "gave birth to her firstborn son; and she wrapped Him in cloths, and laid Him in a manger" (Luke 2:7). Jesus' birth was a human birth.

2. Jesus' life was a *human life.* John testified that Christ became a human being—took upon Himself human nature—and lived here on earth among human beings (see John 1:14). As a man, Jesus possessed all the essential elements of human nature.

As a man, Jesus was controlled by the laws of human development. In infancy and childhood He grew like other children. Luke recorded that Jesus grew physically and mentally, and was loved by God and man (read Luke 2:52). It was necessary for Jesus to make progress physically, intellectually, socially, and spiritually because He was subject to the laws of human development.

As a human being, Jesus experienced all the emotions, limitations, and temptations common to us. Can there be any doubt about this when we consider the witness of the New Testament? The Gospel writers tell of times when Jesus was tired, hungry, and thirsty. Jesus was tired and weary when He sat at Jacob's well (John 4:6). The tears He shed at Lazarus' grave were an expression of the real grief of a sensitive spirit (see John 11:1-34). Jesus felt human sorrow. He needed friends and desired encouragement like any other person. He experienced love, compassion, anger, anxiety, and fear.

Jesus had to fight the same temptations that other people fight. He fought these battles, not only at the beginning of His public ministry when He met Satan in the desert temptations, but to the end of His life. Some people feel that Christ could not have sinned in the temptation experiences even if He had wanted to. If this were so, His victory would have been easy—almost automatic—and would be little comfort to us in our temptation experiences. Jesus' battles against temptation were not merely fought for our benefit. They were real.

3. Jesus' death was a *human death*. His physical suffering on the cross was real. The mental anguish He experienced when His disciples fled was real. The spiritual anguish caused by the feeling that His Father had "forsaken" Him was real (see Mark 15:34). This was not the make-believe play acting of God in human diguise. Jesus was a man—an extraordinary man—whose humanity was undeniable.

As Christians we must hold to the humanity of Christ, because it is crucial for our salvation. If Christ was not fully human, the whole doctrine of redemption falls. "Do you see why?" asked James Stewart. "Suppose we were led to conclude that He was not quite human, . . . not only are we robbed of our most precious pattern and example, but what is far worse, we have to say that God has not come the whole way after all, that God has not quite stooped down to the depth of our urgent need nor borne all our human burden."[2]

When we insist on the full humanity of Christ, we are simply saying that God, in love for you and me, has indeed come all the way. He meets us where we live. He knows all about us and loves us anyway. "There is one mediator . . . between God and men, the man Christ Jesus" (1 Tim. 2:5).

TruthSearch 9

Three facts that point to the humanity of Jesus are:

1. His human _____ .

2. His human _____ .

3. His human _____ .

Was Jesus Fully Divine?

For many centuries before Jesus came to earth, devout Jews had looked for and predicted the coming of the Messiah. The word *Messiah* is Hebrew for "Anointed One." Ideas of what the Messiah would be like and how He would go about His work differed greatly. But expectation that the Messiah would come was widespread.

Do you remember exam day at Caesarea Philippi? Jesus asked the disciples, "'Who do you say that I am?'" And Simon Peter replied, "'Thou art the Christ, the Son of the living God'" (Matt. 16:15-16). The long-awaited Messiah had come in the person of Jesus Christ. The man Jesus of Nazareth was God in human flesh.

We have already affirmed that Jesus was fully, completely, and truly human. We are now ready to affirm that He was fully, completely, and truly divine.

In reading the Gospel accounts, we cannot escape the impression that Jesus Christ is the divine Son of God. There is a sense in which the divinity of Christ can be understood only within the framework of a Christian experience. When we make the commitment to follow Christ and live for Him, we begin to know who He really is. To attempt to *prove* the divinity of Christ to someone who has no interest in the Christian life is often wasted effort. It is within the life of Christian discipleship that we come to a knowledge and appreciation of who Christ really is. Three facts about Jesus point to His divinity.

1. Jesus' birth was a *divine birth*. What would you look for if, at one point in history, God became man? Would it surprise you to learn of mysterious happenings, supernatural events, and a strange mixture of the human and the divine?

If God decided to translate Himself into the language of humanity, it should not surprise us to learn that He would make a special entry into the world of time and space. This special entry we call the virgin birth. Mary asked the angel, "'How can I have a baby? I am a virgin.'"

The angel replied, "'The Holy Spirit shall come upon you, and the power of God shall overshadow you; so the baby born to you will be utterly holy—the Son of God'" (Luke 1:35, TLB). The virgin birth puts the divine and human together.

2. Jesus' life was a *divine life*. Many strange happenings in the life of Christ cannot be explained in human terms. These events present problems only for those whose viewpoint does not allow for miracles or the supernatural. Such people explain away much that happened in the life of Christ. But for those who believe Christ to be the Son of God and the Bible to be a record of His divine activity, no problem exists with the supernatural.

One signpost pointing in the direction of this divine life is the *claim Christ made concerning Himself.* On one occasion, the Sanhedrin, the supreme Jewish council, gathered in the home of Caiaphas, the High Priest, to try Jesus. Caiaphas confronted Jesus with a direct challenge: "'I adjure You by the living God, that You tell us whether You are the Christ, the Son of God.'"

Jesus replied, "'You have said it yourself; nevertheless I tell you, hereafter you shall see the Son of Man sitting at the right hand of power, and coming on the clouds of heaven.'"

The high priest tore his robes and said, "'He has blasphemed! What further need do we have of witnesses? Behold, you have now heard the blasphemy; what do you think?' They answered and said, 'He is deserving of death!'" (Matt. 26:63-66). If Jesus had not made a direct claim to be the Messiah, why was everyone so upset? Somehow on the lips of Jesus this claim seemed entirely fitting, proper, and believable.

A second signpost pointing in the direction of this divine life is the *sinlessness of Jesus.* His friends and enemies turned the brightest searchlights of criticism upon Him without finding one flaw in His moral character. There is no record of Jesus ever confessing personal sin. The writer of Hebrews concluded: "This High Priest of ours understands our weaknesses, since he had the same temptations we do, though he never once gave way to them and sinned" (Heb. 4:15, TLB).

A final signpost pointing in the direction of this divine life is that *Jesus is able to do for people what only God can do.* It is generally accepted that miracles, healing powers, and forgiveness belong to God. Jesus did all this. He performed miracles, healed people, and forgave sin.

Mark, the Gospel writer, told of a time when four friends brought a paralyzed man and lowered him down through a roof right in front of Jesus. When Jesus saw how strongly the men believed that He would help their friend, He said to the paralyzed man, "'Son, your sins are forgiven!'"

But some Jewish religious leaders in the crowd were offended by the fact that Jesus forgave the man's sin. They exclaimed: "'What? This is blasphemy! Does he think he is God? For only God can forgive sins'" (Mark 2:7, TLB).

They were right, of course. Only God *can* forgive sins. But, let's follow the story to its conclusion: "Jesus could read their minds and said to them at once, 'Why does this bother you? I, the Messiah, have the authority on earth to forgive sins. But talk is cheap—anybody could say that. So I'll prove it to you by healing this man.' Then, turning to the paralyzed man, he commanded, 'Pick up your stretcher and go on home, for you are healed!'" (Mark 2:8-11, TLB). The man did as Jesus commanded him.

We are all painfully aware of our need of divine forgiveness. Sin constantly raises a barrier between us and God. What are we to do? Ignore sin and hope the consequences will go away? Remind ourselves that these are only "guilt feelings" not worthy of our attention? No. We confess them to God and claim the divine forgiveness made possible by the death of Christ. Our deepest assurance of divine forgiveness comes when we have encountered Christ. When we experience forgiveness, Christ is doing for us what only God can do.

3. Jesus' resurrection was a *divine resurrection.* The resurrection of

Jesus proves His divine nature like no other event. We have already affirmed His human death. Now we affirm His divine resurrection. The truth is that "Christ died for our sins according to the Scriptures, . . . He was raised again on the third day according to the Scriptures" (1 Cor. 15:3-4).

All four Gospel writers record Jesus' resurrection. The remainder of the New Testament proclaims it. "The bodily resurrection of Jesus is one of the best authenticated events in all of history," concluded Herschel H. Hobbs in *The Baptist Faith and Message*.

To the early disciples—and to many Christians living now—the resurrection was God's stamp of approval on the things Jesus did and said. As history's most extraordinary event, it proved Christ's claim to a special relationship with God.

TruthSearch 10

Three facts about Jesus that prove He was divine are:

1. His divine _____. To me this means:

2. His divine _____. To me this means:

3. His divine _____. To me this means:

Now compare your answers here with those in TruthSearch 9. Why is it important that Jesus was both divine and human?

A Brief Wrap-up

We must conclude that Jesus is both divine and human. The incarnation—the teaching that God became flesh—takes both facts seriously. We must hold to both and give up neither. Why?

Suppose you were asked to cross over a bridge broken only at one end. Would it make any difference which end was broken? No. A bridge broken at either end is inadequate. If Jesus were only a man, we would have a bridge broken on the heavenward end. We could never find God through Him. If Christ were only a phantom-God appearing on the earth without actually becoming man, we would have a bridge broken on the earthward end. In that case we would have no Savior.

Paul asked two questions in his conversion experience. When the risen Christ appeared to him on the Damascus road, the first question he asked was "'Who art thou, Lord?'" (Acts 9:5). We have intended to answer that question in this chapter. After Paul received his answer, he asked a second question, "'Lord, what wilt thou have me to do?'" (Acts 9:6, KJV).

One question logically follows the other. When we fully realize that Jesus is the Christ, the Son of the living God, the only worthy response is to ask, "Lord, what do you want me to do now?"

Honestly Now

Read Matthew 16:13-16. Place yourself in this group of disciples. During the question time you answer the question, Who do your friends say that I am?

TruthSearch 11

Spend a few minutes with your eyes closed. Shut out the world. Be alone with your thoughts. Ask yourself the question, Who would you like Jesus to be to you? Write your answer.

Share these thoughts with God in prayer.

[1]From *The Encyclopedia of Religious Quotations*, edited and compiled by Frank S. Mead (Old Tappan, New Jersey: Fleming H. Revell Company, 1965), 49. Used by permission.

[2]James S. Stewart, *The Strong Name* (New York: Charles Scribner's Sons, 1941) 78. Used by Permission.

[3]Mead, *op. cit.*, 60.

3
About the Holy Spirit

Memory Verses: *John 14:16-17; John 14:26* (cards 6-7)

Some people think that reality is limited to what we taste, feel, smell, see, hear, or bump into. Such a philosophy implies that the Holy Spirit cannot be real because He is invisible. No one has ever captured the Holy Spirit in a test tube. Nobody is going to turn over a rock and discover the Holy Spirit. But does that mean He is not real? Certainly not.

How many times have you seen electricity? Have you ever seen, felt, tasted, or smelled gravity? Isn't it true that our visible world is composed of invisible particles?

TruthSearch 12

How do you know the following are real?

FRIENDSHIP   LOVE

CONSCIENCE   ELECTRICITY

Did you notice that you cannot see, taste, or touch these things? Still, you know they are real, because you have experienced them and have seen their results.

■■ Let's affirm that the HOLY SPIRIT IS REAL. This is a *truth that makes a difference.* I don't understand everything about the Holy Spirit, but that doesn't disturb me.

We begin our search for understanding with a study of the nature of

πνεῦμα

Spirit

The symbol to guide our search is the dove.

We have chosen this symbol because of an event in Jesus' life. At His baptism the heavens were opened, and "he saw the Spirit of God coming down like a dove and lighting on him" (Matt. 3:16, GNB).

A Union of Three in One

Put on your hip boots. Even though the concept is hard to understand, we must talk about the Trinity—the doctrine of the union of three persons (Father, Son, and Holy Spirit) in one Godhead.

In the first two chapters of this book we dealt with the nature of God and the nature of Christ. This chapter on the nature of the Holy Spirit completes our study of the Trinity—God in three persons: Father, Son, Holy Spirit.

The doctrine of the Trinity is a mystery. It cannot be explained completely. Yet, the New Testament clearly presents the fact of the Trinity. WE, THEREFORE, CONFESS THAT THE FATHER IS GOD, THAT THE SON IS GOD, AND THAT THE SPIRIT IS GOD. But we do not believe in three Gods. We believe in one God who relates to human beings in three persons.

Remember, it is possible to affirm our belief in the Trinity while we continue our search into its rich meaning.

Baptists have been protected from various extremes by our balanced theology of Father, Son, and Holy Spirit. These three have always existed and are equal and eternal. A diagram of the Trinity should look like this:

A balanced theology insists on equality. Any time a certain group over-emphasizes one person of the Trinity almost to the point of excluding the other two, the result is extremism.

Extremism

1. Affirming the unity of God

but denying the Trinity

2. Main emphasis on the Son

Father and Holy Spirit made less important

3. Main emphasis on Holy Spirit

Father and Son made less important

Christians who have emphasized the Holy Spirit while giving little consideration to Father and Son have interpreted "the baptism of the Holy Spirit" as separate from conversion. Some people also have practiced speaking in tongues as the proof that a person has received the baptism of the Holy Spirit. In many cases this view has produced emotional excesses, frustration, self-centeredness, and splits in churches. Christians constantly must guard against a "Spiritology" that makes the Father and Son less important than the Holy Spirit.

Healthy Christian theology avoids extremes, keeping the three persons of the Trinity in proper balance. That is, it affirms the equality of Father, Son, and Holy Spirit in the Godhead.

ONE

GODHEAD

How do we explain the mystery of the Trinity? We don't! Illustrations do help, though. One I have found helpful is to compare the Trinity to a drama. Let's think of the Bible as a drama being acted out on a stage. In the Old Testament, the Father is in the center of the stage, while the Son and the Spirit watch from the wings on either side. In the Gospels, the Son is in the center of the stage, while the Father and Spirit are on either side. Beginning with Acts, the Spirit is in the center of the stage, while the Father and Son are on either side. Yet, at all times and in every situation, Father, Son, and Spirit are present and are involved in both the plot and the action.

TruthSearch 13

Which of the following illustrations best helps you to understand the concept of three persons in one Godhead? Circle that one. Then in the space provided write an illustration that has helped you understand the Trinity.

• The Trinity is like an individual with three relationships. One person is a child to his parents, a husband to his wife, a parent to his child.
• The Trinity is like your roles. You are a student, a friend, a teammate. You are one person in three roles.

A Peek at a Person

Have you noticed? It is easier to think of the Father and Son as persons than it is to think of the Holy Spirit as a person. Why? Maybe it's because we have known other fathers and sons who are persons. Have you ever known a spirit who is a person? Some mental effort is needed to accept the Holy Spirit as a person. Let's use that mental effort right now.

The word *spirit* is grammatically in the neuter gender. It isn't masculine or feminine. Usually, we don't consider something in the neuter gender to have personality. But the Holy Spirit does have a distinct personality. He is the third person of the Trinity. He relates to us in a distinct way. Understanding this concept requires some Bible study. Read the following Scripture passages to discover the personality of the Holy Spirit.

Three ways He has shown Himself to people	Genesis 1:2; Matthew 3:16; Acts 1:8
Referred to as a person	John 14:16-17,26; 16:7-15

Things He does:
strives	Genesis 6:3
helps (comforts)	John 14:16-18,26
witnesses (testifies)	John 16:8
convicts (reproves)	John 15:26
guides	John 16:13
gives power	Acts 1:8

Reactions to:
blasphemed	Matthew 24:31
received	John 20:22
resisted	Acts 7:51
grieved	Ephesians 4:30
insulted	Hebrews 10:29

Godlike qualities:
present everywhere	Psalm 139:7
all-knowing	1 Corinthians 2:10
all-powerful	1 Corinthians 12:11

Does God's work:
creates	Genesis 1:2;
provides salvation	John 3:5; John 16:8;
convicts of sin	John 16:8;
gives life	Romans 8:11

Do you need power to live the Christian life in a difficult situation? Do you need power to accomplish a task that is too big for you? Then you need the Holy Spirit. A small group of disciples huddled together in the upper room to wait for the promise of the Father (Luke 24:49). After being empowered by the Holy Spirit, they were told to go out and win the whole world to Christ. The task was too great for them to do in their own strength. They needed the power of the Holy Spirit. That same Spirit will give you power to cope and courage to face *your* impossible tasks.

TruthSearch 14

Recall a seemingly impossible task that you had to face recently. Tell how the Holy Spirit helped you with that task or how He could have helped you if you had asked for His help.

Do you need the ability to effectively communicate your faith to unbelieving friends? Have you longed for the ability to give a testimony that would touch a loved one's heart? Then you need the power of the Holy Spirit. The miracle of Pentecost was one of communication (Acts 2:4-8). Luke observed that the disciples "began speaking in languages they didn't know, for the Holy Spirit gave them this ability" (v. 4, TLB). People of many nations "were stunned to hear their own languages being spoken by the disciples" (v. 6, TLB).

What was happening? Each believer had the ability to tell what God was doing in his life. And every unbeliever had the ability to hear the gospel in a way that he could understand. We desperately need this miracle of communication today.

The Holy Spirit: Alternative to an Empty Life

As a general rule, empty lives do not remain empty. This is the point of an "eerie little parable" Jesus told. It is a story that makes the blood run cold. Ready?

"When an evil spirit goes out of a person, it travels over dry country looking for a place to rest. If it can't find one, it says to itself, 'I will go back to my house.' So it goes back and finds the house empty, clean, and all fixed up. Then it goes out and brings along seven other spirits even worse than itself, and they come and live there. So when it is all over, that person is in worse shape than he was at the beginning. This is what will happen to the evil people of this day" (Matt. 12:43-45, GNB).

Jesus used expelled demons or "evil spirits" to describe the spiritual condition of the people of His day who lived apart from God. Let's describe it for our day. Imagine a person who is sick of the way he has been living. He decides he is going to be different—clean up his life. He drives out the impure spirits and bad habits that have caused his unhappiness. He reforms or turns over a new leaf. Things will be different from now on.

Even impure spirits and bad habits need "a place," however. They come back to see how the young person is doing. They discover that their old house is swept, set in order, decorated, *but empty.* Nothing good has been put in the person's heart and life to replace the evil. They go out and form an alliance with other impure spirits worse than themselves. They return with new force for a complete takeover. The young person is in a worse condition than before.

What was Jesus trying to tell us about life? Empty lives (like empty houses) do not remain empty. Driving out impure spirits and quitting bad habits are not enough. The empty life *will be filled,* either with good or evil.

Too many people live meaningless lives. They have no priorities, no loyalties, and no sense of commitment. Boredom has set in. This condition may be caused by many things, among them a negative kind of religion. Have you noticed the number of people who seem to measure their commitment in terms of what they have "given up" for Christ? In other words, a person is a good or bad Christian in terms of bad habits given up and the list of *don'ts* compiled. But that is not enough! Remember, the main strategy of Satan is not (and never has been) *possession.* His main attack is *temptation.* We need the same power against both.

45

Because empty lives do not remain empty, the Christian invites the Holy Spirit to come in as indweller, possessor, master. Nothing puts the devil to flight like a positive Christian faith. The serious Christian who is well-anchored in his or her faith has a remarkable immunity against the influence of evil.

Your heart was made for divine indwelling. There is a God-shaped vacuum that only He can fill. Jesus said, "Behold, I stand at the door, and knock; if anyone hears My voice and opens the door, I will come in to him, and will dine with him, and he with Me" (Rev. 3:20). The choice is between evil-possession or Christ-possession.

TruthSearch 15

Read John 14:17. Explain what it means to have the Holy Spirit "indwell" you—live in your heart?

Now a Word from Jesus

Jesus taught His followers about the Holy Spirit in His "Farewell Discourse" on the last night before His crucifixion (see John 14:1 to 16:33). At this crucial moment you may be sure that Jesus would say *everything* necessary to help His disciples have a vital Christian experience. Likewise, He would leave out *nothing* that was necessary for them to understand who the Holy Spirit is and what He does.

Five special sayings about the Holy Spirit are recorded in John. Each saying is marked by the repeated use of the title HELPER *(Comforter)*. This term helps us understand how Jesus saw the Holy Spirit. *Helper* or *Comforter* literally means "one called alongside of." The idea is that of a lawyer for the defense or one who pleads another's case. Jesus saw the Holy Spirit as a divine strengthener, encourager, enabler. When He comes into our lives, He helps us overcome weaknesses and enables us to cope.

Open your Bible to John 14 as we discuss the five sayings that Jesus used to describe the person and work of the Holy Spirit. As you read, notice that the work of the Spirit is consistent with the work of the Father. Jesus prays, and the Father gives. The Spirit is "another Helper" of the same kind as Jesus; therefore, what Christ had been to His followers, the Spirit would be after Jesus left earth. The work of Jesus was limited and restricted as to time and place. The Holy Spirit is not limited. He is present everywhere and will abide with the believers forever (v. 16).

Saying 1: "Spirit of Truth" (John 14:15-18). In verse 6 of John 14, Jesus called Himself "the way, and the truth, and the life." Later He presented the Helper as "the Spirit of truth" (v. 17). Christ was the truth about God, revealed objectively in a human life. The Holy Spirit is the truth about God, revealed in Christian experience. The visible companionship (Jesus) has become inner communion (the Holy Spirit). Jesus promised, "I will not leave you as orphans; I will come to you" (v. 18). Many people thought that the crucifixion was the end of Jesus, but He is alive, well, and at work in the lives of people.

We desperately need what the Holy Spirit gives. The greatest problems we face are overcome by the Spirit's presence. The Spirit's promise is: "I will never leave you without a friend. I will come to you." You need never be alone!

Saying 2: Holy Spirit as Teacher (John 14:26). In the second saying, Jesus described the Holy Spirit as our teacher in the school of Christian maturity. Jesus also declared that the Father would send the Holy Spirit "'in My name,'" with full authority to declare the message of Jesus. This means that the ministry of the Holy Spirit always will be consistent with the ministry of Christ. In other words, you may be called on to be a "fool for Christ's sake." But don't do foolish things and blame it on the work of the Spirit.

Christ's intention is that the Spirit as Teacher will do two basic things for us. First, "'He will teach you all things'" (v. 26). The Holy Spirit will continue the teaching ministry of Jesus. The word *disciple* means "pupil" or "learner." Becoming a Christian is an enrollment—not graduation. Jesus made a beginning with us. We have much to learn. It is the Holy Spirit, our Master Teacher, who keeps us wading deeper, farther, on and on. To spend all of your Christian life wading only ankle deep in the spiritual shallows is a tragedy.

In the second place, the Holy Spirit as Teacher will "'bring to your remembrance all that I [Jesus] said to you'" (v. 26). The Spirit continues to bring to remembrance things we have let slip. Most of the time we need reminding more than informing.

One of our problems in living as a Christian is ignorance. We cannot blame God though. He has given us the Holy Spirit to help us overcome this problem. Have you asked the Holy Spirit to be your Teacher in the school of Christian maturity?

TruthSearch 16

Write about an experience when the Holy Spirit helped you to understand a new truth about God or learn the meaning of a particular Scripture passage.

Saying 3: Holy Spirit as Witness. The mission of the Holy Spirit is stated in the third "Helper" saying (John 15:26-27). His work is to magnify Jesus: "'He will bear witness of Me'" (v. 26).

An interesting question emerges at this point. When I claim the presence of the Holy Spirit, will I magnify spiritual gifts I have received? Will I magnify myself or will I magnify Jesus? The supreme test of things attributed to the Spirit is, Do these things magnify Jesus?

When the story of Jesus is told, the Holy Spirit assures us that it is truth. This is witness from the divine side. The individual Christian also is commissioned to magnify Jesus: "'You will bear witness also'" (v. 27). This is witness from the human side.

The Holy Spirit's presence is the answer to life's most pressing problems. Do you lack power when you witness to unbelievers? Do you find yourself trying to accomplish spiritual goals in the power of the flesh? "My problem is lack of power," you say. Have you claimed the power of the Holy Spirit? This is our wonderful privilege.

TruthSearch 17

The power of the Holy Spirit enables us to choose actions that magnify or bring positive attention to Jesus. Tell about a time when the Holy Spirit helped you witness about Jesus.

Saying 4: Holy Spirit as Cross-Examiner (John 16:5-11). In the fourth "Helper" saying, we are introduced to the Holy Spirit as the cross-examiner of the unbeliever. These verses answer the question, What may we expect the Spirit to be doing in the life of the unbeliever?

Jesus began this section with some amazing words. "'It is to your advantage that I go away'" (v. 7). Can you imagine? All our lives we have wished for the opportunity to see Jesus. We would like to ring His doorbell and ask Him a few questions. How could it possibly be to our advantage that Jesus go away? Let's hear Him out: "'For if I go not away, the Helper shall not come to you; but if I go, I will send Him to you'" (v. 7). Jesus was going away in a visible, bodily sense (limited by time and space). He would return in the person of the Holy Spirit, no longer limited by time and space. Now He is able to influence *all* people in *all* places at *all* times.

The Holy Spirit has a special assignment with regard to the unbeliever. "'And, He, when He comes, will convict [convince] the world concerning sin, and righteousness, and judgment'" (v. 8). He will cross-examine the unbeliever until he sees and openly admits his sin.

Have you ever tried to convince someone that he or she is a sinner? You failed, right? Convincing is the work of the Holy Spirit. We must permit Him to do His work. First, He convicts people of their sin, "'because they do not believe in Me [Jesus]'" (v. 9). When men first crucified Jesus, they did not believe that they were sinning. Later, the crucifixion was preached and they were "pierced to the heart" (Acts 2:37). How do you explain the difference? The Holy Spirit was doing His work.

The Holy Spirit also convinces the unbeliever of righteousness, "'because I go to the Father'" (John 16:10). When people first looked at the cross, it appeared that righteousness had failed. Later, a centurion looked at the same cross and said, "'Truly this was the Son of God!'" (Matt. 27:54). How do you explain the difference? Could it be that the Spirit was at work?

Finally, the Holy Spirit convinces people of the certainty of judgment, "'Because the ruler of this world [Satan] has been judged'" (John 16:11). When people first looked at the cross, they thought Jesus had been judged and condemned. Later they saw that, in reality, it was Satan himself who had been judged and condemned. How do you explain the difference? The Holy Spirit was doing His work.

The Holy Spirit provides what we need most. For the unbeliever He provides the evidence of sin that brings the conviction necessary for conversion. For those of us who are His witnesses, He goes before us to convince or convict the unbeliever of his need for conversion. To convince people that they are sinners is the Holy Spirit's work—not ours.

TruthSearch 18

How did the Holy Spirit help you understand that you were a sinner and that you needed to turn your life over to Jesus?

Saying 5: Holy Spirit as Living Presence (John 16:12-15). In the last "Helper" saying, the Holy Spirit is presented as the living presence of Christ for today's world. Jesus expressed a dilemma that every Christian teacher feels at one time or another, "'I have many more things to say to you, but you cannot bear them now'" (v. 12). Apparently, the disciples were not mature enough at this point for some truths. God reveals to us only as much as we can understand and put into practice.

If some truth is being deliberately withheld—to be revealed to Jesus' disciples at a later time—how will it be revealed and whose responsibility will it be? The answer is found in verses 13-15. The Holy Spirit, the living presence of Christ, will continue and complete the training Christ began. Their work is the same. Their authority is the same: "'He will not speak on His own initiative, but whatever He hears, He will speak'" (v. 13). Their purpose is the same: "'He [the Spirit] shall glorify Me [Jesus]'" (v. 14). Their teaching is the same: "He takes of Mine; and will disclose it to you'" (v. 15).

The Holy Spirit is not to be thought of as an agent acting independently of and apart from Christ. He is working jointly with and dependent on Christ. The ultimate outcome of their work will be the same. If you are involved in some activity that is not consistent with the life and teachings of Jesus, do not blame it on the Holy Spirit.

Tying Up Loose Ends

In the five "Helper" sayings, we have examined what Jesus said about the Holy Spirit. He was speaking on the night before His crucifixion. At that crucial moment, Jesus explained clearly who the Holy Spirit is and what He does.

We need what only the Holy Spirit can give. Let's do a brief recap on what the Holy Spirit is to the believer. Here is what we can expect Him to do for us:

He gives personal power (Acts 1:8).
He gives boldness in witnessing (Acts 4:8-13).
He is our divine Counselor (John 14:1 to 16:33).
He takes up permanent residence within us (John 14:17).
He is our personal teacher (John 14:26).
He is our instructor to complete the training Christ began (John 16:12-15).

That's not bad for a beginning! The possibilities are unlimited.

TruthSearch 19

Which of the six ministries of the Holy Spirit listed in the previous paragraph do you need most right now? Write a prayer telling God about your need.

Honestly Now

My purpose in this chapter has been to explore the doctrine of the Holy Spirit. My hope is that the Spirit will be more real and, therefore, more believable to you now. When the Spirit comes into focus for you, your spiritual life will take on more meaning.

The Holy Spirit is a person. Our relationship to Him is a personal one. The Spirit is the member of the Trinity *who teaches us.* As Paul said, "The love of God has been poured out within our hearts through the Holy Spirit who was given to us (Rom. 5:5).

4

What Is God's Purpose for People?

Memory Verses: *Psalm 8:5-6; Romans 7:22-23* (cards 8-9)

We now turn our attention to a study of the nature of

ἄνθρωπος

man

The symbol of our search will be . .

In the previous chapters we affirmed God's desire to be known and His revelation of Himself in His Son, Jesus Christ, and through the Holy Spirit. But why all this interest in people? Why would God go to so much trouble to be known by human beings?

The psalmist had the same question in mind when he observed: "When I look at the sky, which you have made, at the moon and the stars, which you have set in their places—what is man, that you think of him; mere man, that you care for him?" (Ps. 8:3-4, GNB). What is God's purpose for people? We are all looking for the answer to that question.

■■ I BELIEVE THAT EACH HUMAN BEING IS A CREATURE OF WORTH. For me, *this is a truth that makes a difference.* I don't pretend to understand all the complex factors of human nature. Neither do I pretend to understand all the mysteries of God's dealings with people. But, that doesn't disturb me.

Remember, it is possible to affirm our belief in the worth of the individual while we continue our search for greater understanding of the nature of people.

TruthSearch 20

Write one brief sentence stating your understanding of God's purpose for people.

_____

Now write a sentence describing what you think is God's purpose for you. Be specific.

_____

Life is an amazing blend, harmony, and integration of body, mind, and spirit. The human being is a combination of the physical, the psychological, and the spiritual. To be a human being is difficult and complicated. There is some question as to whether the human race is up to the challenge.

As a Christian today, you are living in confusing times. The field of knowledge is expanding with breathtaking speed. The future becomes the present so rapidly it leaves us in a state of shock. Determining our purpose in life takes great effort.

Homo Sapiens or Homo Mechanicus?

Is a person a human being or a human machine? Is a person determined by his past or free to choose against his past? Does environment and heredity determine a person's choices, or is each individual responsible for his or her behavior? Answering these questions is crucial in understanding human nature.

Individuals are exposed to numerous fields of knowledge which, in varying degrees, support the idea that people function as machines. Within these fields a person is considered a creature of law, a victim of heredity, or a product of environment. Carried to extremes people become objects or robots, without human value and prone to fatalism. This view allows no freedom for God to interact with a person and no room for personal responsibility for chosen behavior.

One of the great dangers of this age of science, technology, specialization, and professionalism is that we may lose our sense of the importance of the person. People may be reduced to robots, statistics, cogs in a massive wheel, a file folder, a number, or a card in a roll book.

Most of us have experienced the empty feeling that follows being dehumanized—treated as less than human. We resist automatic lives, robot-like movements, and the treadmill of meaningless activity where no one takes the slightest interest in us *as persons*.

The twentieth century introduced a new problem—the population explosion. Wall-to-wall people are everywhere. Yet, the irony is that people are lonely. In the middle of great crowds of people, one person can live isolated in unbelievable spiritual solitude.

We affirm while we search. We know, but we don't know. At times we are confused by our own actions. We are not as bad as we could be; nor are we as good as we should be. This journey toward self-discovery is lifelong. Along the way we will experience both the low moments of discouragement and the high moments of rich personal satisfaction.

Answers to the question, Who am I? are numerous. Recent thinkers have swayed masses of people by their views of personhood that recognize no Godward dimension. Darwin understood and explained human beings under biological categories. Nietzsche insisted that people are governed by impulse and instinct. Marx equated the idea of man with the ideal of society. Freud saw people as essentially sex instincts. As a result of these views, people have marched fearlessly backward to a worship of blood, power, and sex that is similar to the situation in pre-Christian days. With the Godward dimension missing, the words *responsibility* and *accountability* are also missing from human behavior.

We must admit that we are wonderfully made and very complex. On one hand, we are obviously influenced by our past. There is a sense in which past experiences influence present behavior. On the other hand, the Christian gospel insists that we are free to choose against or rise above our past. Present behavior is not dictated or determined by past experience. A person is constantly aware of the freedom to choose.

One individual described the paradox: "The thing that amazes me about human beings is the goodness of some pretty bad people and the surprising badness of some otherwise good people."

TruthSearch 21

Give an example of a pretty good bad person:

Now give an example of a pretty bad good person:

The field of great literature repeatedly reveals the complex nature of human personality. People are continually torn between two worlds. Robert Browning commented, "Men are not angels, neither are they brutes." Ralph Waldo Emerson said, "Man is a god in ruins. . . . Every man is a divinity in disguise, a god playing the fool." The noted American humorist Will Rogers observed, "God made man a little lower than the angels, and he has been getting a little lower ever since." Blaise Pascal spoke of man as "a confused chaos! . . . the glory and the scandal of the universe!"[1]

Are People Essentially Good or Evil?

Belief in the essential badness of people is easy to establish. We are born with an inclination toward sin. Later, when the option of choosing good or evil is before us, we deliberately and willfully choose the way of sin. Paul concluded that "all have sinned and fall short of the glory of God" (Rom. 3:23).

When we look within our own lives, we find further proof that all have sinned. We are amazed at the gap between what we are and what we ought to be. Sometimes we are even afraid of ourselves, afraid of the forces at work within, and afraid of the actions that we feel ourselves capable of carrying out. While the doctrine of depravity does not mean human beings are totally bad, it does mean a person is limited, unfinished, sinful, and if left to himself, not capable of much progress.

The purpose of William Golding's book *Lord of the Flies* is to expose this basic defect in human nature. What will become of a person left entirely to himself without any authority or restraint? What is the result of "doing what comes naturally"? What if every individual "did his own thing"? What might we expect?

Golding told of a small group of English boys brought up in nobility, who were fleeing atomic warfare. Their plane crashed on a lonely island. The pilot died in the crash.

These boys faced existence without adult influence. On this island there were no parents, no schools, no policemen. Consequently, there was a complete absence of law, authority, and discipline. They had to establish a new order. What would they do?

Ralph began to emerge as leader. He used a shell as a megaphone to call meetings. He served as a constant reminder of what the boys had been and ought to be. He symbolized past experience and common sense. He became the conscience of the group.

Piggy was a short, fat boy with thick glasses. He was an intellectual and served as a reminder of the place of reason in establishing a new order. He was treated as an outsider and was gradually rejected by the group. In a struggle late in the book, Piggy's thick glasses were broken, symbolizing the final break with intellect. Piggy was ultimately killed by the group.

As the story progressed, Jack emerged as leader of the hunters. At first he innocently hunted and killed pigs for food. Then he developed a love for killing. Before the story ended he had painted his face and, behind this mask of liberation, became a bloodthirsty savage.

At first the boys felt an uneasiness in their wrongdoing. Ralph tried in vain to keep a fire going. No one was interested enough in being rescued to help him. Things began "breaking up," "going rotten." Rules were rejected without concern. Savages emerged. They began to live like animals. There was no message from the grown-up world.

On one occasion Ralph said to Piggy, "What's wrong with us? What makes things break up like they do?" Later on, the "Lord of the Flies" (a translation for the Hebrew word for devil) explained to Simon, the mystic, "'You knew, didn't you? I'm part of you? Close, close, close! I'm the reason why it's no go. Why things are what they are.'"[2]

Finally Jack (the savage) began to hunt Ralph (the conscience of the group) to kill him. About that time a ship landed on the island. Ralph ran and wrapped his arms around the British naval officer's legs. The captain looked at the wild, painted savage hunters and said: "'I should have thought that a pack of British boys—you're all British, aren't you?—would have been able to put up a better show than that' . . . And Ralph wept for the end of innocence."[3]

TruthSearch 22

How true to life do you think *The Lord of the Flies* is? Why?

On the other hand, there is considerable opinion and much evidence that *people are good*. The average person does not think of himself as a sinner. He thinks of himself as a fairly good person who, now and then, makes a mistake. He thinks of God as an indulgent, heavenly being standing by to forgive.

Looking in certain areas, considerable optimism concerning humanity can be found. Sometimes this optimism is overinflated. A rewritten version of Psalm 8 is one example of this viewpoint: "O man, how excellent is thy name in all the earth! Who hast set thy glory above the heavens . . . When I consider thine inventions, the work of thy fingers, the aeroplanes and atomic bombs which thou hast made, what is God that I should be mindful of him, or the Son of God, that I should reverence him?"[4]

We must resist all efforts to make man a god in disguise. The author of Psalm 8 had an exalted view of man because he had an exalted view of God. Our understanding of human nature is largely determined by the kind of God we have.

While some people insist that people are made "a little higher than the beasts," the psalmist proclaimed that God has made man" "a little lower than the angels" (Ps. 8:5). Or, as the Revised Standard Version translates it a "little less than God." We must resist any idea that people are merely the highest form of animal life giving expression to natural passions and impulses. On the other hand, we must resist any concept that makes man a god deserving praise for his human achievements. The glory belongs to God—not humankind.

TruthSearch 23

Psalm 8:5-6 is printed below with all the nouns, pronouns, and a few other words missing. Fill in the missing words and memorize the verses.

"Yet _____ hast made _____ a little lower than

_____ , And dost crown _____ with

_____ and _____ !

_____ dost make _____ to rule over the

_____ of _____ _____ ; _____

has put all _____ under his _____ .

How do you feel . . .

knowing that God made you like Himself—in His image (Gen. 1:27)?

knowing that God has put you and others in charge of His creation?

What Does the "Image of God" Mean?

In the biblical view, human beings are not simply the highest form of animals; they are special creations of God. A person is not merely a physical and mental machine; he is also "spirit and soul and body" (1 Thess. 5:23), because he has been created in the image and likeness of God. "Then God said, 'Let us make man in our image, according to our likeness;' . . . and God created man in His own image, in the image of God He created him; male and female He created them" (Gen. 1:26-27).

What does it mean to be created in the image of God? People are different, unique, special creations of God. They have a distinct kinship with the Maker. They can communicate with God. They are capable of thinking God's thoughts after Him. They have a sense of right and wrong. They can express emotions. They can rejoice in the things in which God rejoices. The greatest wonder, short of God, is the mind of a human being.

The image of God in a person has nothing to do with physical image. We are not God's look-alikes. It was established in chapter 1 that God is spirit (see John 4:24). This means, among other things, that God is invisible. He cannot be seen by the human eye. God does not have a physical body with human characteristics.

What distinguishes the God of the Bible from the divinities of other religions is that He is a personal God who speaks personally to people. What distinguishes people from the rest of created beings is that they are capable of fellowship with other persons and of communication with a personal God.

God created you as a person of worth. God is interested in you. He cares what happens to you. He is for you and not against you. His basic stance toward you is a stance of love. As a person, created in the image of a personal God, you possess tremendous potential. You will be held accountable for this potential.

TruthSearch 24

Read Genesis 1:27 again. Explain the meaning of being made in the image of God.

The Dilemma

So far we have established that people are basically good and evil. They have an amazing capacity to be both.

This struggle between good and evil continues after a person becomes a Christian. On one hand is the lower nature constantly pulling downward toward a life of sin and selfishness. On the other hand, the higher nature constantly draws us upward toward a life of selflessness and spiritual victory.

R. Lofton Hudson described the lower nature as the "man in the basement." This secret self, aggressive and untamed, is constantly trying to break out and demands constant watching. The more the "man upstairs" (conscience) is controlled by the Spirit of God, the more the Christian will be victorious over the "man in the basement" (lower nature). "But the whole problem of salvation and Christianity," concluded Hudson, "is bringing this man in the basement under control and into cooperation with God."[5]

We take a giant step toward spiritual maturity when we accept the tension between the lower and higher nature as a lifetime struggle. Every Christian will experience decisive spiritual victories won by faith in Christ. Christians must never assume, however, that past victories vaccinate them against constantly recurring battles and struggles with the man in the basement.

Paul tried to warn us that the new life in Christ is no snap. Speaking naturally and sincerely out of his experience, Paul described the civil war raging within him: "We know that the law is spiritual; but I am unspiritual, sold as a slave to sin. I do not understand what I do. For what I want to do I do not do, but what I hate I do. And if I do what I do not want to do, I agree that the law is good. As it is, it is no longer I myself who do it, but it is sin living in me" (Rom. 7:14-17, NIV).

Paul had to admit that there were times when he didn't even understand his own actions. The struggle continued: "I know I am rotten through and through so far as my old sinful nature is concerned. No matter which way I turn I can't make myself do right. I want to but I can't. When I want to do good, I don't; and when I try not to do wrong, I do it anyway" (Rom. 7:18-19, TLB). Does this struggle sound familiar?

Many people argue that Paul was describing his condition before he became a Christian—not after. Just to be honest, I am aware of the conflict Paul described as a present, continuing fact in my Christian experience. Aren't you?

TruthSearch 25

Read Colossians 3:5-9,12-17 to note some "basement" characteristics and to discover new life qualities that God can substitute for the "basement" characteristics.

Old-Life Characteristics   New-Life Replacements

Most of us identify with Paul's description of the dilemma: "It seems to be a fact of life that when I want to do what is right, I inevitably do what is wrong. I love to do God's will so far as my new nature is concerned; but there is something else deep within me, in my lower nature, that is at war with my mind and wins the fight and makes me a slave to the sin that is still within me. In my mind I want to be God's willing servant but instead I find myself still enslaved to sin. So you see how it is: my new life tells me to do right, but the old nature that is still inside me loves to sin" (Rom. 7:21-23, TLB).

Paul felt as though he were a split personality, two men in one skin, a walking civil war. You and I have felt this often. We are never as good as we know we ought to be. Is there any hope then? Or, do we just give up and sin boldly?

The Christian life can be a victorious life. Paul discovered a reason for hope when he said, "What an unhappy man I am! Who will rescue me from this body that is taking me to death? Thanks be to God, who does this through our Lord Jesus Christ!" (Rom. 7:24-25, GNB). Our deliverance may be partial and incomplete now because of the continuing influence of the lower nature, but victory is possible! Christ is the resource for victory in the Christian life.

Salvation does not deliver us completely and entirely from the lower nature. Growth toward Christian maturity consists in continuing submission to the Spirit's control and in the strengthening of our conscious controls. The living presence of Christ within strengthens our inner resources against temptation. Christ saves the whole person, but the "man in the basement" is not completely destroyed. The lower nature must be kept under control by the Spirit of God working through the Christian. The more we submit to the control of the Holy Spirit, the more we are able to control our aggressive, untamed impulses. The more we submit to the influence of the lower nature, the more our lives are characterized by sinful and selfish behavior.

The Christian wins victory after victory, but he never quite destroys the enemy. Those who continue to struggle against temptation are growing spiritually. Those who give up are pathetic. Only in the future is our victory really complete. Only in heaven will we be completely delivered from the presence of sin and the impulses of our lower nature. Present victory is possible only as we submit to the control of the Spirit. And, Christ does expect us to be victorious!

The Answer to the Dilemma

It has been said that we would rather die than really be known. Nevertheless, I am convinced that the true nature of a person is really worth knowing. Since human beings are created in the image of God, we possess a potential and purpose that we must understand and appreciate.

A person has potential for both bad and good. He may be converted to the unworthy as well as to the worthy. When a person persists in going his own way, things do fall apart and go rotten. Selfish living results in lost direction, destiny, or purpose. Knowing much about pleasure, we know little about joy. Knowing much about ease, we know little about peace. What is left is a "God-ache" in the heart. We have discovered by personal experience the necessity of conversion.

A person's greatest potential lies in freedom of choice. That is what makes an individual responsible before God. God loves us too much to violate our freedom to choose. Jesus declared: "'Heaven can be entered only through the narrow gate! The highway to hell is broad, and its gate is wide enough for all the multitudes who choose its easy way. But the Gateway to Life is small, and the road is narrow, and only a few ever find it'" (Matt. 7:13-14, TLB). The choice is yours.

TruthSearch 26

Underline the phrase in Romans 7:14-25 that best describes you. Tell why you selected that phrase.

Talk with God about your struggle to live His way.

This is the good news: Human nature can be changed! Lives are being changed. This is our hope! People are becoming new creations; old things are passing away; all things are becoming new (see 2 Cor. 5:17). A person does not have to go on like he is. Miracles continue to take place.

What is meant by conversion? We are talking about that process, gradual or sudden, by which an individual commits the direction of his or her life to God's leadership. It is a total surrender to God's will; a total dedication of oneself to God. Conversion is accepting fellowship with Christ as life's highest good. It is a deliberate and willing choice to be a follower of Jesus Christ.

When conversion takes place, Jesus does not take our humanity away from us; He comes down into it, so that we can bring our temptations and failures to Him. This helps us maintain our fellowship with Him. The next chapter deals with what happens in conversion.

Honestly Now

Describe the war going on within you. _____

_____

_____

What are your areas of greatest conflict? _____

_____

_____

Make a list of qualities and traits that you would like to have in your life. Ask God to help you work on cultivating these qualities.

---

[1]From *The Encyclopedia of Religious Quotations,* edited and compiled by Frank S. Mead (Old Tappan, New Jersey: Fleming H. Revell Company, 1965) 288-96. Used by permission.

[2]William Golding, *Lord of the Flies* (New York: Capricorn Books, 1959) 192. Used by permission.

[3]Ibid. 186.

[4]A. C. Craig, *Preaching in a Scientific Age* (New York: Charles Scribner's Sons, 1954), 72. Used by permission.

[5]R. Lofton Hudson, *Helping Each Other Be Human* (Waco: Word Books, 1970) 152. Used by permission.

[6]Mead, *op. cit.,* 292.

5

What Happens in Conversion?

Memory Verses: *John 3:5-6* (card 10)

Debbie was a bright-eyed fifteen-year-old. Had I been able to pick her brain, I would have discovered mostly question marks. She had not attended church much. Her knowledge of the Bible was skimpy. She came to the point abruptly: "I don't understand this conversion stuff. And why do you have to be baptized?"

The next thirty minutes were spent in laying a foundation for Christian conversion. We discussed such questions as: Why is conversion necessary? What happens in conversion? What does it mean to be a Christian? The purpose of this chapter is to explore with you the questions I discussed with Debbie.

We continue our search for truth with a study of the meaning of being

γεννηθῇ ἄνωθεν

born again

The symbol to guide us will be the cross.

■■ A person's greatest need is to have a vital relationship with God through Jesus Christ. I BELIEVE THAT, THROUGH THE CONVERSION EXPERIENCE, A VITAL RELATIONSHIP WITH GOD IS MADE POSSIBLE. This is a *truth that makes a difference.*

Remember, it is possible to affirm our relationship to God through the conversion experience while we search for greater understanding of being born again.

Let's Define Our Terms

Words mean different things to different people (*happiness,* for example). Part of our problem in describing the process of becoming a Christian is the words we use. Often, we use words that do not communicate. We may have some great ideas, but what is their value if we cannot put those ideas into words that people can understand?

The word *salvation* is probably the word used most to describe conversion. It is an all-inclusive word that describes the total experience. Some people speak freely of "being saved" or "getting saved" and feel sure lost persons understand. Do they? Do these words communicate to the unbeliever?

In the Old Testament the basic idea behind the word *salvation* is deliverance from the problems and difficulties of life. The emphasis in the New Testament is primarily on salvation from sin. The angel assured Joseph concerning Mary: "'She will bear a Son; and you shall call His name Jesus, for it is He who will save His people from their sins'" (Matt. 1:21).

The New Testament word for *salvation* comes from the verb which means "to restore to health" or "to make whole." Salvation is an experience that makes us whole spiritually. The sick woman, who in faith touched the hem of Jesus' garment, was "made whole" (literally, saved). (See Matt. 9:20-21.)

Another word that needs defining is *regeneration.* This word describes salvation from the divine side, or what God does for a person. Regeneration is the inner change brought about by the Holy Spirit. It is the new birth described by Jesus in John 3:3-7. The new birth is the "divine head start" that the Spirit can give to every person.

Once again words may mean different things to different people. Jesus told Nicodemus, "You must be born again."

"'Born again!' exclaimed Nicodemus. 'What do you mean? How can an old man go back into his mother's womb and be born again?'" (John 3:4, TLB).

See the problem? Jesus was talking about spiritual birth. Nicodemus was hearing physical birth. Even Jesus, the Master Teacher, had problems with communication.

The final word is *conversion,* the one used in the title of this chapter. This word describes salvation from the human side or the outward evidence of the inner change. Conversion is that process, gradual or sudden, by which a person commits the direction of his or her life to God's leadership. Conversion is a deliberate and willing choice to be a follower of Jesus Christ.

TruthSearch 27

Pretend you are talking to someone your own age who has never been in church. Describe the following experiences, using no "churchy" or "theological" words.

SALVATION:

CONVERSION:

Is Conversion Really Necessary?

Some people seem to live happy, well-adjusted lives without conversion. Our friend Debbie questioned the need for this experience. Are we to assume that conversion is for everybody? If so, why? What makes conversion necessary? The answer requires a brief review of biblical history. Hang on tight. What follows is the Bible in a nutshell.

The Bible assumes that God exists. He is a holy and just God. In the process of time, He created the universe and human life. As the crowning act of creation, human beings were made "in the image of God" (Gen. 1:26-27). As emphasized in chapter 4, what distinguishes human beings from the other created beings is that a human being is able to communicate with God and to have fellowship with other persons.

So far, so good. The holy God created people capable of fellowship and response. He could have made people like puppets, but puppets cannot return love. Because He wanted people capable of love, God took a great risk. He gave them freedom of choice. This means that a person is free to love God—or not love Him.

God had high expectations for the people He had created. He longed for perfect fellowship and a good relationship with them. God desired for people to be holy as He was holy. Then sin entered the picture. A person exercised freedom of will and *chose against God*. Humanity fell short of what God intended—and that was sin.

One of the favorite New Testament words for sin is a word that means "to miss the mark." You draw the bow. The arrow speeds through the air, falling to the ground before reaching the intended target. It falls short of the goal. In comparison, sin is falling short of God's ideal of righteousness. Paul wrote, "All have sinned and fall short of the glory of God" (Rom. 3:23).

OK, a holy God has sinful humanity on His hands. What will He do with them? God must be true to His own nature. His holiness includes both justice and love. What can He do to bring sinful people back and, at the same time, be true to Himself? Let's look at the possible solutions that were available to God.

In the first place, God could have *measured out punishment in exact proportion to a person's sin.* The measuring stick could have been "an eye for an eye, and a tooth for a tooth." Let every person pay the penalty for his sins. This approach would have put justice in the spotlight while ignoring love. God could not accept this alternative and be true to His nature.

As a second alternative, God could have *taken sin lightly and forgiven all people,* whether or not they desired forgiveness. In this case He would have adopted a policy of leniency condoning and "winking at" sin. He could have relaxed the standards and excused His favorites. "Well, sin really isn't all that serious," He could have said. But this approach would have put love in the spotlight while ignoring justice. God could not accept this alternative and be true to Himself.

Only one choice remained. God must be just. People are guilty, and there is a penalty: "The wages of sin is death" (Rom. 6:23). The penalty must be paid. But, God is also a God of love. How can He express His love for the sinner while showing His dissatisfaction with the person's sin? *Well, He could pay the penalty Himself!* In so doing, justice would be satisfied because the penalty for sin would be paid. Also, love would be manifested in that God paid the penalty He demanded.

This leaves people with the freedom of choice. They are free to accept or reject God's plan. God loves us too much to violate our freedom to choose. He places the choices before us and waits: "See, I have set before you this day life . . . and death, blessing and curse; therefore choose life, that you and your descendants may live" (Deut. 30:15,19, RSV).

TruthSearch 28

Explain why conversion is necessary.

Why Did Jesus Have to Die?

Our need to be forgiven is obvious. But why did Jesus have to die on the cross so that God could erase my sins? If God is all-powerful, surely He could have taken care of sin another way.

In Old Testament days, God's chosen people had difficulty accepting the idea of a Suffering Servant (Isa. 53:1-12). In New Testament times, Jesus' own disciples raised their voices in shocked disapproval when He spoke of His approaching death. Then the cross became history. Since that time, the unbelieving world has pointed with scorn at a Savior who had to die. All the while, the Gospel writers kept saying the cross was a working out of God's eternal purpose.

Our salvation was within God's purpose. It was God's intention to bring sinful humanity back into right relationship with Himself. On the cross, God got under the burden of our sins: "God was in Christ, reconciling the world to Himself" (2 Cor. 5:19).

The concept of Jesus' death on the cross is not easy to grasp. Human reasoning balks at the idea. Do you mean that God takes our sins so seriously that He came to be crucified—by us—for our sins against Him? Do you mean that God loves us so much that He "gave His only begotten Son that whoever believes in Him should not perish, but have eternal life"? (John 3:16). Not bad!

Why did Jesus have to die? Perhaps an illustration will help. Let's suppose there is a judge in our town who has a reputation for being both just and loving. A rare combination, indeed. When people are brought before him, they can always count on his fairness and love. However, he has made enemies on both sides because, at times, he has been "too just" or "too loving" to suit people's fancy.

One day a dear friend of the judge was brought before him for trial. His crime was described. His guilt was proved. Everyone knew about the penalty for such misconduct. What would the judge do? He couldn't be lenient, even though the man was a close friend. He couldn't be harsh in assigning the penalty because of his love for the man. Everyone wondered how he would respond. His enemies thought they finally had him in an impossible situation.

The judge rose from the bench and declared that his friend was guilty. He went on to describe the penalty in the form of a fine. Then, he took off his robe, stepped down from behind the desk, and paid the fine for his friend.

The cross accomplished the same balance of justice and love. People were sinners—guilty as charged. Everyone was aware of the penalty for sin. But God had a reputation for being both just and loving. What would He do? He declared humankind guilty. He described the penalty for sin. Then, He took off His royal robe and stepped down from heaven to earth. On the cross He paid the penalty He Himself demanded.

A familiar example illustrates vividly what the cross was all about. A notorious criminal was in jail at the time Jesus was crucified. He was charged with murder and insurrection. One day he heard the steps of the guard outside his cell. The key turned in the lock, and the door swung open. The guard said firmly, "Come with me."

They walked together up a narrow, dark corridor. The prisoner became fearful. "Where are you taking me?" he asked.

Calmly the guard replied, "You have been set free."

In disbelief the criminal said: "Come on, man! Don't joke about something so serious. Is my execution set for today?"

The guard responded matter-of-factly: "I am serious. You have been set free. Another has paid your penalty. Another will die in your place. You may go now."

Barabbas stepped out into the fresh air and bright sunlight—a free man.

TruthSearch 29

Using the following form, write a "non-poet's poem" that expresses your feelings about Jesus' sacrifice for you:

JESUS DIED FOR ME

_____ _____

(two verbs describing Jesus' action)

_____ _____ _____

(three adjectives describing Jesus' death)

_____ _____ _____ _____

(four-word phrase about Jesus' death)

_____

(word that means the same as Jesus' death)

Concerns About the Conversion Experience

We know that conversion marks the point when a person makes a commitment to follow Christ. But what should we expect the conversion experience to be like? This question raises other questions, such as Does it happen all at once? How does it feel to be saved? Is emotion always involved? How can you turn your life over to God? Let's look at three concerns that relate to these questions.

The first concern relates to *what kind of experience a person should expect to have*. When he was fourteen, Richard had confessed faith in Christ and was baptized. A few months later he confided to a youth worker that he was not sure he had been converted. When the friend probed about the reason for his lack of assurance, Richard said, "What happened to me was not anything like what Judy described when she got saved." He doubted, because his experience was not like what others described.

Let's establish one fact as a starter: no two conversion experiences are exactly alike. People are different. Some show their feelings more than others. Some by nature are calm and composed. You see this at a ball game. Two spectators sit side-by-side. One sits quietly and calmly throughout the game. The other jumps, yells, cries, and screams. But they both *experience* the game.

A second concern about conversion relates to *gradual or sudden conversions* to Christianity. To hear some people talk you would think their conversion was an "on-the-spot" decision with no prior thought or exposure. Others describe an experience that is a gradual awakening, like the small bud that slowly opens into a full-grown flower. Both experiences are possible.

TruthSearch 30

What concerns do you have about your conversion experience or your anticipated conversion experience? Write them.

In what way was your conversion experience different from:

The eunuch:

Saul:

The Philippian jailor:

How does your daily living reveal that you have accepted Christ as your Lord and Savior?

The Bible records many different kinds of conversion experiences—all of them genuine. Let's look at three experiences recorded in the Book of Acts. The Ethiopian eunuch was the treasurer from North Africa, a man of great authority under the queen. He was searching for truth. When Philip read to him from the Book of Isaiah and told him about Jesus, the eunuch responded immediately. His decision was calm and deliberate. He said, "'Look! Water! What prevents me from being baptized?'" (Acts 8:36).

Saul, on the other hand, seemed far from being a Christian. In fact, he was busy persecuting Christians. On the road to Damascus he met Jesus face-to-face. He saw a bright light and heard the voice of the risen Christ speaking to him. In that one dramatic moment the entire direction of his life was changed—from persecutor to preacher. Not every conversion is that dramatic. Read about his conversion in Acts 9:1-21.

In the Philippian jailer we witness the conversion of a pagan who had very little background for Christianity. He heard Paul and Silas praying and singing at midnight. He trembled with fear when he thought they had escaped. Upon learning that they were still within the dungeon (when they could have escaped), he said, "'Sirs, what must I do to be saved?'" (Acts 16:30).

They replied, "'Believe in the Lord Jesus, and you shall be saved'" (Acts 16:31). He believed and was baptized (see Acts 16:22-36).

Each of these conversions is different. Yet, each is genuine. We can't wait around trying to create an experience that is like someone else has described. Nor can we insist that everyone else have an experience exactly like ours. We must allow God to be original with every person. God wants originals—not carbon copies.

The final concern about conversion relates to *the time and place of the conversion experience.* Many people are able to tell you the exact date, time, and place of their commitment to Christ. Others sometimes are disturbed by the fact that their experience was more gradual. They know they are followers of Christ, but they cannot be specific as to time and place of commitment.

An illustration may help dispel the confusion. Falling in love may be either sudden or gradual. For some couples it is love at first sight. Most people discover that the experience is more gradual. They grow into love. The day they always remember is their wedding day—not the day they fell in love. Their anniversary is an annual celebration of the day they stood at the altar and said, "I do." Regarding conversion, the day remembered by most Christians is the one on which they made their public commitment or were baptized.

Age at the time of conversion may be a factor in remembering the experience. A person saved at a young age may not remember the exact time and place while a teenager or adult may have the time and place details clearly in mind.

To know the when and where of your conversion is helpful. But the most important proof is "the fruit of the Spirit" borne in the daily life as evidence that Christ lives within.

Where Do We Start?

Every journey must have a beginning. The traditional starting point for the Christian *is within the church.* When Melanie came to me, she was a walking bundle of problems. In the course of our talking together I asked her if she were a Christian. Her reply was typical: "Well, I suppose so. I am a member of First Baptist Church." Some people assume they are Christians simply because they are members of a church.

I love the church and have given my life to service through it. At the same time, I recognize that a person is not automatically a Christian because he is a church member. The church is made up of converted people, but it is not a saving institution. Christians are usually committed to the church, but commitment to the church does not make a person a Christian.

The same is true of baptism. When I asked Gary about his relationship to Christ, he said: "I guess I'm not a Christian. I haven't been baptized yet."

The church is made up of baptized people, but baptism did not bring them into a right relationship with God. You may ask, "If one has been baptized and has joined the church, isn't that fairly good proof the person is a Christian?" Maybe yes. Maybe no.

Many people believe they are Christians (or not Christians) on the basis of *the way they feel.* Thomas said: "When I first became a Christian, I had this happy, 'out-of-the-world'-feeling. Now I feel sad, depressed, and ashamed. I guess I'm not a Christian anymore."

Haven't you noticed how fickle and changing feelings are? A Christian experiences a wide variety of feelings. Anyway, I have never found in the Bible a statement describing how we are supposed to feel when we are saved. People are different. Some feel more deeply than others. Some are hurt more easily than others. Both joy and sadness come in a wide variety of colors. If our emotions swing like a pendulum, would God accept them as trustworthy proof of our salvation?

I have good news! Your relationship to God is not based on feeling. At the moment you trusted Christ, you became a "child of God." That was the beginning point of a continuing and permanent relationship with God.

TruthSearch 31

Since being baptized and joining a church doesn't save a person . . .

Why should a Christian be baptized?

Why should a Christian join a church?

Who Is a Christian?

Followers of Christ have been called by many names: disciples, saints, followers of the way. "And the disciples were first called Christians [Christ-ones] in Antioch" (Acts 11:26). The name *Christian* was a label given them by their enemies. What did it mean then? What does it mean now? These questions are related to the basic question, What happens in conversion?

In the following paragraphs is a discussion of two basic statements that describe what happens in every true conversion. These two elements are absolutely essential. Are you a Christian? Let's see.

First of all, a Christian is *one who has "come to himself."* The best illustration of what this means is found in a parable that Jesus told—the story of the runaway boy or the lost son (see Luke 15:11-24). When the story begins, we recognize the seeds of rebellion. The boy rebelled against the restrictions of home and the repression of external authority. He grew tired of his father stepping in with house rules. He wanted to be free.

The boy developed dreadful fear—the fear that he would not taste life to the fullest. He decided to become his own boss. He took what was his and left home.

In a far country he fulfilled his supreme ambition—to do as he pleased. The excitement soon wore off. Everything went horribly flat. Aimless boredom set in. He began to hear the rattle of invisible chains. His situation went from bad to worse. His quest for freedom ended in abject slavery. And bitter laughter went up from the pig pen.

The boy began to compare his present and former conditions. Thoughts of his father's house made it difficult to be satisfied with the pig pen. He also began to look at himself. He didn't like what he saw. At this point, Jesus said that the boy "came to himself." The door was open for repentance—a complete change of mind.

He decided to go back home. His attitude toward home, father, and freedom had changed greatly. The boy was willing to say to his father, "'I have sinned against heaven and in your sight'" (Luke 15:21). He found the father watching and waiting—as we always do.

A person realizes that he has failed, and he comes to a new understanding of his real need. Repentance is the result—a complete change of mind about God, sin, and personal responsibility.

Second, a Christian is *one who has come by faith to accept Jesus Christ as Savior.* Coming to Christ is absolutely necessary to the Christian life (see Matt. 11:28-30; John 1:11-14; Acts 16:30-34; Rom. 10:8-13; 2 Tim. 1:12). Salvation happens when we, by faith, come to God in the name of Jesus Christ. We come to Christ believing that God will do what He has promised.

What does it mean to be a Christian? It means at least three things. It means we have entered *a new life.* Jesus spoke of the "new birth" which begins this new spiritual life (John 3:3-7).

Being a Christian also means we have *a new relationship.* We have a new relationship with other Christians. This new family relationship is called the church. You need the church, not to bring you into right relation to God, but to help you grow to maturity in the Christian faith.

Finally, being a Christian means we have *a new life-style.* Accepting new conduct does not make you a Christian, but becoming a Christian should make a difference in the way you live. The Christian experience is a life-time process of putting the teachings of Christ into practice in our daily lives.

TruthSearch 32

Draw a ring around words and phrases in the puzzle that name the following:

- TWO ESSENTIAL ELEMENTS for true conversion
- THREE RESULTS of true conversion

```
C N E W R E L A T I O N S H I P Q W R T Y P S D F G G
O G T R Z X C V N M L F H G J R W Q S X V N C M L Y Y
M A C C E P T S J E S U S C H R I S T A S S A V I O R
E T Y D J C N V B M X Z P R W Q L K J S D G H R Y P T
T R T Y L N E W L I F E F G H R O D P L W Y S D R M B
O R W H I M O M R W T I L O V E Y O U Y O C P B C M M
S G H Y Q C M S O B Y S M I L E P L M N B W R T S X X
E G S C Q P Z C S S S R Q W R T Y P S D F G H J K L L
L R T Y P L K J H G F D O N E W L I F E S T Y L E W M
F M Q N W R B T V Y C X P Z L X K J C H V G B F N D M
```

See page 94 for answers.

Honestly Now

Are you a follower of Christ? If not, there must be a beginning. Your falling in love with Christ may have been either gradual or sudden. But the time has come for you to say, "I accept Christ as my personal Savior and Lord."

---

[1]Mead, *op. cit.*, 292.

6

What's So Special About the Bible?

Memory Verse: *2 Timothy 3:16* (card 11)

Another vital area of our search for truth will be the

βίβλος
Bible

The symbol of our search will be the scroll.

■■ I BELIEVE THE BIBLE IS GOD'S SPECIAL WORD TO PEOPLE. This is a *truth that has made a tremendous difference* in the direction of my life. I'll have to admit that parts of the Bible are difficult for me to understand, and some of it may always remain a mystery. But, that doesn't disturb me. I take the Bible seriously, because it is God's true and inspired Word.

Remember, It is possible for us to affirm our belief in the Bible as the Word of God while we continue our search for a greater understanding of the unsearchable and inexhaustible riches within its pages.

The War Within
Romans 7:22-23, NASB

For I joyfully concur with the law of God in the inner man, but I see a different law in the members of my body, waging war against the law of my mind, and making me a prisoner of the law of sin which is in my members.

9 Doctrine—People

Born Again
John 3:5-6, NASB

Jesus answered, "Truly, truly, I say to you, unless one is born of water and the Spirit, he cannot enter into the kingdom of God. That which is born of the flesh is flesh, and that which is born of the Spirit is spirit."

10 Doctrine—Conversion

Inspired Writing
2 Timothy 3:16, NASB

All Scripture is inspired by God and profitable for teaching, for reproof, for correction, for training in righteousness.

11 Doctrine—Bible

Pray Always
1 Thessalonians 5:16-18, NASB

Rejoice always; pray without ceasing; in everything give thanks; for this is God's will for you in Christ Jesus.

12 Doctrine—Prayer

Fellowship
Acts 2:42, NASB

And they were continually devoting themselves, to the apostles' teaching and to fellowship, to the breaking of bread and to prayer.

13 Doctrine—Church

From Death to Life
Romans 6:4, NASB

Therefore we have been buried with Him through baptism into death, in order that as Christ was raised from the dead through the glory of the Father, so we too might walk in the newness of life.

14 Doctrine—Baptism

In Remembrance
1 Corinthians 11:26, NASB

For as often as you eat this bread and drink the cup, you proclaim the Lord's death until He comes.

15 Doctrine—Lord's Supper

His Coming Again
John 14:3, NASB

"And if I go and prepare a place for you, I will come again, and receive you to Myself; that where I am, there you may be also."

16 Doctrine—Last Things

Fellowship Acts 2:24	The War Within Romans 7:22-23
13 Church	9 People
From Death to Life Romans 6:4	Born Again John 3:5-6
14 Baptism	10 Conversion
In Remembrance 1 Corinthians 11:26	Inspired Writing 2 Timothy 3:16
15 Lord's Supper	11 Bible
His Coming Again John 14:3	Pray Always 1 Thessalonians 5:16-18
16 Last Things	12 Prayer

God Is Spirit
John 4:24, NASB

"God is spirit, and those who worship Him must worship in spirit and truth."

1 Doctrine—God

God Is Light
1 John 1:5, NASB

And this is the message we have heard from Him and announce to you, that God is light, and in Him there is no darkness at all.

2 Doctrine—God

God Is Love
1 John 4:8, NASB

The one who does not love does not know God, for God is love.

3 Doctrine—God

Jesus the Messiah
Matthew 16:16, NASB

And Simon Peter answered and said, "Thou art the Christ, the Son of the living God."

4 Doctrine—Jesus

Word Became Flesh
John 1:14, NASB

And the Word became flesh, and dwelt among us, and we beheld His glory, glory as of the only begotten from the Father, full of grace and truth.

5 Doctrine—Jesus

The Spirit of Truth
John 14:16-17, NASB
"And I will ask the Father, and He will give you another Helper, that He may be with you forever; that is the Spirit of truth, whom the world cannot receive, because it does not behold Him or know Him, but you know Him because He abides with you, and will be in you."

6 Doctrine—Holy Spirit

The Spirit, Our Teacher
John 14:26, NASB

"But the Helper the Holy Spirit, whom the Father will send in My name, He will teach you all things, and bring to your remembrance all that I said to you."

7 Doctrine—Holy Spirit

People, God's Creations
Psalm 8:5-6, NASB

Yet Thou hast made him a little lower than God, And dost crown him with glory and majesty! Thou dost make him to rule over the works of Thy hands; Thou hast put all things under his feet.

8 Doctrine—People

Word Became Flesh
John 1:14

God Is Spirit
John 4:24

5 Jesus

1 God

The Spirit of Truth
John 14:16-17

God Is Light
1 John 1:5

6 Holy Spirit

2 God

The Spirit, Our Teacher
John 14:26

God Is Love
1 John 4:8

7 Holy Spirit

3 God

People, God's Creations
Psalm 8:5-6

Jesus, the Messiah
Matthew 16:16

8 People

4 Jesus

The Bible has been called the least-read, best-selling book in the world and "The Book Almost Nobody Reads." To say the least, we purchase it more than we read it, and we praise it more than we study it.

The Bible is a special Book and should have a vital place in the life of every believer.

Special in Its Revelation of God

How would you like to recieve a personal message from God to guide you in dealing with your problems and to help you make sense out of life? Most of us would appreciate that. May I tell you where you can find such a message? The Bible is a message from God addressed especially to you. If you read it faithfully and take it seriously, God will speak to you through its pages, just as personally as if He had sent you a letter.

The Bible has been called God's love letter to human beings. It contains answers to the basic needs of every heart. The Bible is God's chosen instrument through which His word is spoken directly to us.

Kierkegaard remarked, "We don't read the Bible; it reads us." It reads us like an open book. The Bible is a special Book because it helps us to know who and how we are.

The central theme of the Bible is God's disclosure of Himself. Sometimes this revelation came through His encounter with a single individual. At other times it involved the nation of Israel as a whole. As you read the Bible, remember that these were real people in a real world who had undergone real experiences with a real God.

TruthSearch 33

Choose the statement about the Bible that you like best and tell why:

"The Bible is God's love letter to human beings."

"We don't read the Bible; it reads us."

"The Bible helps us know who and how we are."

"The Bible tells about real people in a real world who had undergone real experiences with a real God."

Special in Its Makeup

Would you like to understand the Bible better? That should be the ambition of every believer. If you seriously want to hear the voice of God speaking to you through the Bible, you must be willing to read it and to study it carefully on a regular basis.

Understanding the makeup of the Bible as a whole is a good place to begin. The Bible is a collection of many books. Though it comes to you as one Book with one binding, it is, in reality, a library of sixty-six different books. It has been written by many different authors under different circumstances over a period of more than 1200 years.

Three different languages were used in writing the Bible: Hebrew, Aramaic, and Greek. The authors were from a variety of backgrounds, and they addressed their books to many types of situations. This means that each book must be understood as a unit.

In a real sense, however, the Bible is one Book. Like the human body, the variety of its parts compose one beautiful unity. This unbelievable unity in the Bible can be explained in one way: the God who reveals Himself has one primary purpose—the redemption of all people.

The Bible has two main divisions, called the Old and New Testaments. The word *testament* means covenant or will. The Old Testament is primarily the book of the Jewish religion and contains God's covenant with His people before Christ came to earth. The New Testament is the book of the Christian religion and contains God's new covenant with His people made possible through Christ. The final authority on Christian living is found in the New Testament.

The Bible contains many different kinds of literature. You will understand it better if you know the type of literature you are reading. Are you reading prose or poetry? Are you reading history or drama? Are you reading law or prophecy? Are you reading a letter or apocalyptic literature (like Revelation)?

Perhaps you are reading a passage that reflects the Hebrew fondness for picturesque, figurative, and symbolic language. Any high school English teacher will tell you that the rules for interpretation change with the nature of the literature.

Studying the Bible can be an exciting adventure. To illustrate, use your imagination. Imagine that the Bible is a beautiful building made up of sixty-six rooms. You have been invited to take a tour. The Holy Spirit will be your guide as you tour the King's Palace. This tour will move at a fast pace. Later you can come back and spend as much time as you like in each room.

First, you enter the spacious entry room of Genesis where you are introduced to the God of creation. Just ahead are the law courts and a side

wing containing the picture gallery of the historical books—scenes of battle, portraits of brave men, and trophies of travel.

Then enter the schoolrooms. One room is marked "Philosophy" with Job as teacher. Another room, marked "Musical Conservatory," is used for a study of the Psalms—some of the best poetry set to music in all the world.

The upstairs contains a business office where the Book of Proverbs governs procedure. Around the corner is the research department headed by brilliant Solomon. The text is Ecclesiastes.

Up on the deck is the observatory where the major and minor prophets peer through a powerful telescope, not so much up into space as down through time, looking for the appearance of the new Star.

Downstairs and across the courtyard, you come into the throne room of the King Himself. Matthew, Mark, Luke, and John introduce you to Him who is King, Servant, Man, and yet God. You will want to come back often to that room. There is so much to see!

Next, enter the workshop of the Holy Spirit—the Book of Acts. In this workshop He is busy making new individuals and a new church and developing plans for world conquest.

Through an open door, see the correspondence office. In there a number of men, under the personal direction of the Spirit of Truth, are busy writing letters to young churches.

Just before the tour ends, the guide pulls some drapes aside permitting you to glance into the unveiling room with a window toward the future. Here you see revelations of glory, adoration, and praise, and catch a glimpse of a new heaven and a new earth.

My hope is that you will come back often to this beautiful building for lengthy visits with a prayer for understanding and guidance.

TruthSearch 34

Complete each statement by supplying the missing item(s).

The Bible was written in the following languages: _____ ,
_____ and _____ .

The Bible has _____ books; yet it is _____ Book.

The two main divisions of the Bible are the _____
_____ and the _____ _____ .

The Bible contains the following types of writings:

     law   prophecy   biography

   history   _____   _____

If you weren't able to fill in all the blanks, read the previous section again to find the answers.

Special in Its Nature

If God is to speak to us through the pages of the Bible, we must have a better understanding of the nature of the Bible. Someone has said that the Bible is a revelation *of* God, *from* God, *to* man, *through* man. This statement reflects the mysterious blend of the divine and human elements in revelation. God speaks to us in the Bible through human authors and human words.

Why God has chosen to communicate through the pages of this particular Book is a question that Christians cannot answer. The fact that God does speak through the Bible is a matter of universal testimony.

God chose to present His message through human personality. He used about forty men as authors in the writing of the books of the Bible. The writer of Hebrews testified to this use of human means to communicate God's message: "Long ago God spoke in many different ways to our fathers through the prophets, . . . telling them little by little about his plans" (Heb. 1:1, TLB). Peter also stated that men spoke from God: "For no prophecy was ever made by an act of human will, but men moved by the Holy Spirit spoke from God" (2 Pet. 1:21).

When the Bible was written, God worked in the same way He has always worked: namely, through human beings like us. No wonder the Bible throbs with the heartbeat of humanity. No wonder it is called the drama of human life.

The authors of the Bible were carefully selected and possessed certain qualifications. Yet, they were not robots or stenographers. Each man had his own writing style and was free to express his own personality in the writing under the leadership of the Holy Spirit. For example, the purpose of the four Gospel accounts is to cover basically the same materials—the life of Christ. Yet, each Gospel is distinctly different and reflects the literary style of its author. Consider also the writings of John and Paul. Both were theologians. Yet, their writing styles are widely different. Each wrote in his own way under the controlling power of the Holy Spirit.

The Bible is special because it is divinely inspired. To be a Baptist is to be committed to the Bible as the primary authority in matters of faith and practice. The reason for this is simple. The Bible itself contains numerous claims that suggest its unique inspiration.

To emphasize the divine inspiration of their message, the prophets constantly used the phrase "Thus saith the Lord." An Old Testament passage that indicates God's direct involvement in revelation is Exodus 24:12: "The Lord said to Moses, 'Come up to Me on the mountain and remain there, and I will give you the stone tablets with the law and the commandment which I have written for their instruction.'"

Even though no formal definition of inspiration is given in the Bible, the

fact of divine inspiration is found often. In the New Testament Paul declared in the second letter to Timothy: "The whole Bible ('literally, Every Scripture') was given to us by inspiration from God and is useful to teach us what is true and to make us realize what is wrong in our lives" (2 Tim. 3:16, TLB).

The word *inspiration* means "inbreathed." To *inspire* means to "breathe into." In expiration, life goes out. In inspiration, life comes in. By inspiration, then, we mean that the Holy Spirit worked through the human spirit of the writers, guiding the process. The writers were "inbreathed" or inspired by God to write. Peter explained that the Holy Spirit within godly men gave them true messages from God (see 2 Pet. 1:21).

It should not surprise us that the Bible emerges as a Book with both divine and human elements: divine because it is inspired by God; human in the sense that God chose to present His message through human personality.

Inspiration, the teaching that God inbreathed or inspired the writers, takes seriously both the divine and human elements in the Bible. We must hold to both and give up neither. Why? Because if we erase the divine element, we argue against the witness of the centuries that the Bible is the Word of God. If we erase the human element, we disregard the divine use of human personality for the communication of that Word.

TruthSearch 35

Match the items to note facts about inspiration of the Scriptures.

_____ 1. inspiration
_____ 2. prophets' declaration
_____ 3. divinely inspired
_____ 4. 2 Timothy 3:16
_____ 5. 2 Peter 1:21

a. writing guided by Holy Spirit
b. all Scriptures inspired by God
c. "inbreathed" by God
d. reason Bible is special
e. "Thus saith the Lord"

Special in Its Preservation

Carol asked, "How can we say that these sixty-six books are the only inspired books of the Bible?"

Who put the Bible all together? When? On what basis were some books omitted? Have you ever wondered about some of these details? The time will come when you will want to do a careful study of these questions. Resources are available. For now, let me make a few brief observations that might be helpful.

The most remarkable event in the history of literature is the fact that the sixty-six books of the Bible, written by forty or more men over a period of more than 1200 years, were preserved and ultimately brought together into one great Book. Our view of inspiration must be broad enough to include the process of preservation. The hand of God was at work preserving these precious writings.

The sixty-six books selected for the Bible form what is called the canon of the Scriptures. The word *canon* means "to measure." These selected writings had to measure up to certain qualifications or meet certain tests. The choices were based on long, careful, and prayerful investigations. We can be sure that each book included in our Bible has passed certain tests and has proved itself to be a part of the inspired Word of God. Other books written during this time fell short of these tests and were rejected. The process of selection was completed by AD 400.

Sometimes, it comes as a shock when people learn that we do not now possess the original manuscripts of any of the books in our Bible. The original manuscripts have long since perished. However, we do have certain very old manuscripts of the books of both Testaments. They are old enough to be accurate copies and are of tremendous value. These manuscripts are preserved in libraries around the world and are guarded with the greatest care. Recent finds, such as the Dead Sea Scrolls, have provided abundant evidence that the writings we now have are substantially the same as in the days of the first Christian century.

Once again, our theory of inspiration must include preservation. As God was involved in the process of the writing of these books, so was He involved in the process of their preservation until they were brought together in our Bible as we have it today.

Special in Its Purpose

How can God speak His message to us unless we understand the purpose of the Bible? The Christian who wishes to become a good Bible student must recognize the primary purpose of the Bible.

Primarily, the Bible is a Book of religion. The nature of its message is religious. The central concern of the Bible is with man's relationship to God, God's relationship to man, and man's relationship to his fellowman.

One purpose of the Bible is *that persons might believe.* John made this purpose clear when he wrote, "These have been written, that you may believe that Jesus is the Christ, the Son of God; and that believing you may have life in His name" (John 20:31).

The unbeliever should search the Scriptures because they testify of Jesus. They tell how we come into right relationship with God. In the Bible God makes Himself known to the unbeliever as a loving and forgiving God. The unbeliever begins to experience life when a sorrow for sin develops and he or she turns in faith to Christ. Faith is developed and encouraged by listening to and reading the Word of God (see Rom. 10:17).

A second purpose of the Bible is *that believers might grow.* So you are a Christian. Now what? Peter urged, "Like newborn babes, long for the pure milk of the word, that by it you may grow with respect to salvation (1 Pet. 2:2).

A baby is not born walking, talking, and eating meat. We must teach a baby to walk one step at a time and to talk one word at a time. We start the baby on milk and soft foods; the steak comes later.

When one becomes a Christian, that person is a newborn babe in Christ. A new Christian doesn't mature overnight. It takes time and effort to learn how to walk and talk as a Christian. The new convert should crave the genuine milk of the Word of God, because it will help one grow in the Christian faith. The steak will come later.

The church does not expect a new convert to be a full-grown Christian overnight. Experience has taught us that the maturing process takes time. When you fail, your Christian friends will be standing by, not to criticize, but to give encouragement.

The Bible is one of our main resources for Christian growth. In a farewell message to the Ephesian elders (Acts 20:32), Paul said: "'And now I commend you to God and to the word of His grace, which is able to build you up and to give you the inheritance among all those who are sanctified [set apart for God's service].'"

Someone has pointed out that, physically speaking, there are three-stages in the maturing process. In the first stage we are fed by others. Our growth is entirely dependent on what others do for us. We move into the second stage when we learn to feed ourselves. We are no longer completely dependent on others. The final stage comes when we assume responsibility for feeding others.

You are already beginning to see how this applies to the spiritual life. In our spiritual development we must all go through stage one. For a time our spiritual growth will depend largely on what others do for us (our pastor, Sunday School teacher, or a Christian friend).

It is a great day for everyone when we enter stage two where we begin to assume responsibility for feeding ourselves. At this time we begin to read the Bible because we want to, not because of outside pressures. We begin to pray because we enjoy fellowship with God, not because some-one is standing by urging, "Say your prayers." We begin to go to church, not because parents insist, but because we desire to worship God and to fellowship with His people. And, when we are not growing as we should, we begin to put the blame where it really belongs (on us), and not on "the youth program of the church."

We have reached the final stage in the maturing process only when we begin feeding others. We now have spiritual children who have come to know Christ through us. They are in stage one and are dependent on us for their growth.

The maturing process takes time. God becomes concerned when we get "locked in" at one stage and stop growing. The writer of Hebrews described this common problem: "You have been Christians a long time now, and you ought to be teaching others, but instead you have dropped back to the place where you need someone to teach you all over again the very first principles in God's Word. You are like babies who can drink only milk, not old enough for solid food. And when a person is still living on milk it shows he isn't very far along in the Christian life, and doesn't know much about the differences between right and wrong. He is still a baby-Christian! You will never be able to eat solid spiritual food and understand the deeper things of God's Word until you become better Christians and learn right from wrong by practicing doing right. Let us stop going over the same old ground again and again, always teaching those first lessons about Christ. Let us go on instead to other things and become mature in our understanding, as strong Christians ought to be" (Heb. 5:12 to 6:1, TLB).

TruthSearch 36

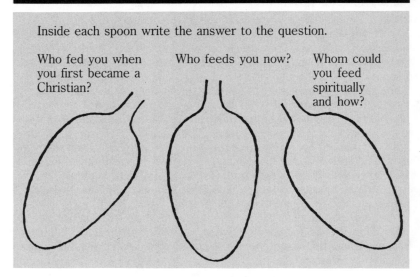

Inside each spoon write the answer to the question.

Who fed you when you first became a Christian?

Who feeds you now?

Whom could you feed spiritually and how?

How Should This Special Book Be Studied?

Most of us would agree that we ought to study the Bible. In fact, it is absolutely impossible to be the right kind of Christian unless we take time regularly to expose ourselves to the Word of God. Yesterday's food will not sustain us indefinitely; malnutrition is a spiritual as well as a physical problem.

I wish I could offer you a simple formula for Bible reading that would guarantee spiritual growth, but that is not possible. Some people read the Bible without much observable difference taking place in their lives.

Is it possible to be a Bible reader and still not be a good Bible student? The answer has to be *yes*. Many Christians have developed habits of Bible reading which, if used exclusively, will not result in a mature understanding of the Bible. These habits may not be bad or harmful. They are just inadequate if they represent the only method or approach for Bible reading.

Let me mention some of these inadequate approaches, giving them humorous titles to aid the memory. They have been collected over many years from numerous sources.

First is the *Santa Claus* approach. The person who uses this approach will spend hours reading the Bible, searching for the surprise element. He will exhaust time and energy on unimportant details that do not result in spiritual maturity. He will try to impress you with all the unusual and sensational "goodies" he has in his bag. This person may be a baby Christian, but you will never catch him up short. He knows the facts!

Next is the *Jigsaw Puzzle* approach. The one who uses this method is the casual "Scripture-nibbler." This person jumps around from one part of the Bible to another, without plan or purpose. While reading she will take a piece from here and a piece from there and try to put them together to mean something. By using this method, she can make the Bible say anything she wants.

Then, there is the *Magic Book* approach. In this approach the only time a person goes to the Bible is when he is facing a baffling problem or a difficult decision. He lets the Bible fall open at random and a verse "leaps out" at him and serves as an answer to his immediate problem or decision. Many people give unusual testimonies to the effectiveness of this approach. My point is that an individual will never become a serious Bible student by using this method exclusively.

Others use the *First Aid Manual* approach. In this case the Bible is used for emergencies only. It is placed on the shelf alongside Dr. Spock's books. When certain spiritual ailments are confronted, the Bible is pulled down, and the concordance is used to find verses that prescribe a cure.

Finally, there is the old *Rabbit in the Hat Trick* approach. By this method a person puts the rabbit into the hat when no one is looking, and later brings it out, to the surprise and delight of the onlookers. Some people have called this the reverse action approach to Bible study. The process is simple. An individual first determines what she wants to believe. Then, she goes to the Bible to find selected verses that "prove" her viewpoint.

TruthSearch 37

Which inadequate Bible approach are you most prone to use?

Read the rest of this section. Why is this a better Bible study approach than any of those just described?

Someone has suggested that there are basically two types of Bible readers: (1) those who read *into* the Bible what they want it to say, (2) those who read *out of* the Bible what it actually has to say.

If you wish to become a serious Bible student, there is a price you must be willing to pay. Casual "Scripture-nibbling" will not enable you to reach that goal. You must be prepared to *read* the Bible and to *study* it with plan and purpose.

The goal of the serious Bible student is to discover the mind and purpose of the original writer. It is only in discovering what the Bible *meant* that we also discover what it *means*. You can understand the Bible. You only need to be a sincere seeker after truth.

Nothing is quite as suspense-filled and breathtaking to me as the first-hand experience of mountain climbers. How would it be if we approached the task of Bible study with such determination? Both mountain climbing and Bible study require *teamwork*. In Bible study and in mountain climbing there is great value, at the start, in climbing with a group of experienced climbers. For a while, success may depend on skillful and experienced teachers who are willing to help others understand the Bible. The Bible study programs in our churches are committed to group study with experienced climbers.

Both mountain climbing and Bible study also require *special equipment.* The person who is serious about Bible study will need some basic tools. The first step up toward serious study may be as simple as buying a translation that you can understand. Word usage and meaning have changed greatly since the King James Version was translated in 1611. Bible study has taken on a new dimension for many people simply by the purchase of a recent translation. A good study Bible that you could obtain is *DiscipleYouth Bible.* In addition to being an easily understood translation, it contains some helpful Bible-study aids, along with a Bible concordance.

The next piece of Bible-study equipment you will need is a one-volume

commentary on the entire Bible. A commentary will give you the historical background needed for understanding each book. You will discover
such details as authorship, dáte, purpose of writing, to whom the book
was written, and the nature of literature you are reading (see pp. 2b—
12b in *DiscipleYouth Bible*). The meaning of many passages of Scripture
will remain hidden until you have this information.

You also will need a Bible dictionary. This resource will enable you to
look up words and study the grammar, especially in passages that are
difficult to understand. By looking up certain names and places you will
gain insight into the world of the Bible.

A guide for Bible study is another helpful tool. This resource explains
Bible study methods.

These various tools will aid you in understanding the environment and
purpose of the writer. Only after you have discovered the original setting
are you ready to determine the original meaning.

In both mountain climbing and in Bible study, there are *overwhelming
obstacles* to overcome. The first thing you will notice is that some parts of
the Bible are easier to understand than others. For that reason you may
want to begin with books such as Luke, John, and Acts. Then, read the
rest of the New Testament, leaving Revelation until last. Just as the tender-
foot mountain climber does not begin with Mount Everest, the Bible student
does not begin with Revelation.

Later, as your skills develop, be prepared to "camp out" indefinitely in
those places in the Bible where the going gets rough. Also, be prepared
for times of spiritual drought and extreme exhaustion.

TruthSearch 38

On the mountain, write four Bible-study tools that can help you get to the top:

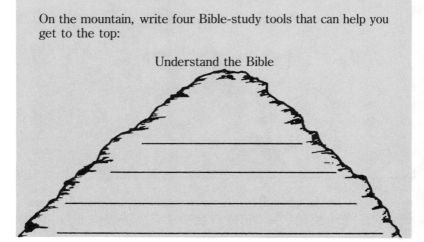

Understand the Bible

In both mountain climbing and Bible study, *the goal is always the top*. In Bible study, however, the top is never clearly defined. In fact, new peaks are always before us. We are continually facing the "unsearchable riches" of God's Word. Nevertheless, we experience the joy of progress in our understanding of the Bible. Whatever discipline is involved, the reward makes it worthwhile.

There is one basic difference in Bible study and mountain climbing. We will never experience the sadness of the mountain climber—sadness because a great adventure has ended. The task of the serious Bible student is a never-ending one.

Honestly Now

Do you study your Bible as much as you should? Write out a Bible reading goal. Then list plans to help you reach this goal. Pray that God will help you work your plan.

---

[1]From *The Encyclopedia of Religious Quotations*, edited and compiled by Frank S. Mead (Old Tappan, New Jersey: Fleming H. Revell Company, 1965), 73. Used by permission.

Answers to Truth Search 32: Come to yourself; Accepts Jesus Christ as Savior; New Relationship; New Life; New Lifestyle.

7

To Pray or Not to Pray

Memory Verses: *1 Thessalonians 5:16-18* (card 12)

Every Christian needs to develop and practice spiritual disciplines. Just as the physical body improves through regular exercise, nourishment, and discipline, so does the spiritual life. For that reason the Christian must always take seriously certain spiritual disciplines—Bible reading, Bible study, prayer, church attendance, and fellowship with other believers. Developing strong, good habits will help get rid of the weak, evil habits in our lives.

The spiritual discipline we will now seek to understand is

προσευχή

prayer

The symbol of our search will be . . .

■■ My affirmations about prayer are simple: (1) I DO PRAY, and (2) I BELIEVE PRAYER MAKES A DIFFERENCE. At the same time I admit I do not understand all that is involved in prayer.

Remember, it is possible to affirm some truths while we continue our search for deeper understanding of the purpose and power of prayer.

What Is Prayer?

Is your life meaningless at times? Do you become bored? Do you ever lose heart? Jesus suggested that Christians "at all times . . . ought to pray and not to lose heart" (Luke 18:1). When you are tempted to give up, you always have the option of choosing to pray for God's guidance and strength.

What is prayer? Most of us begin with the idea that prayer is talking with God. Sounds simple enough.

After a time of talking with God, prayer may take on a new dimension. We can begin to realize that prayer is a two-way communication. It is more conversation with God than it is a monologue. Prayer is *listening* as well as *talking*. In prayer we actually are seeking to bridge the gap between the human and divine. As you mature in your Christian life, prayer can become a personal, daily fellowship with a God who loves and cares for you. It is constant conversation and personal communion.

Late one evening during a retreat David rattled the door of my crude cottage and asked, "When you pray, how can you be sure it is God answering and not just your wishful thinking?" I had no easy answer for David's question.

Basically we rely on the promises of the Bible concerning prayer. God has chosen to communicate with most of us through the "still, small voice" that speaks directly—but without words—to our conscience. The result is a quiet, calm assurance that "This is the way. Walk in it."

Prayer is not pious, empty words piled up so that we can say we have had our quiet time. Simply saying "prayer words" is not enough. Sincerity is more valuable than fancy words. I find some people responding favorably to what is called "conversational prayer." This is an effort to be completely honest and open with God. The result is short, sentence prayers in everyday language. The "Thee's," "Thou's," and church words are omitted. Try this type of praying. You will like it.

Prayer has been called "the breath of the soul." I like this comparison.

Prayer is as necessary to the spiritual life as breathing is to the physical life. But, carry it one step further. We don't get up in the morning, take one deep breath and make it last all day! Breathing is a constant, consistent process. Nor are we to get up in the morning, say a hasty five-minute prayer and make it last all day! Prayer should become a way of life for us—as natural as breathing. Prayer is the attitude of mind and the atmosphere in which we live. How else do we understand Paul's advice that we "pray without ceasing" (1 Thess. 5:17)?

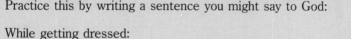

TruthSearch 39

One definition of "pray without ceasing" is to ask and heed God's guidance for every word you say and every action you take. Practice this by writing a sentence you might say to God:

While getting dressed:

While riding the school bus:

While taking a test:

While talking to a friend with a problem:

While meeting someone you want to impress:

During a stiff competition:

Does Prayer Make a Difference?

"I tried prayer for a while," Mary said. "But I must not be talking to God in the right way or something. It doesn't seem to do any good."

Some people insist that *prayer cannot do anything.* They say prayer cannot possibly make a difference, because the universe is governed by inflexible and unchanging laws. This is God's world, and His will is bound to be done anyway. What possible difference could it make whether I pray or not?

For such people, the world is like a traffic light. It operates by certain laws. Its changes are planned and timed. The personal desires of the automobile driver or pedestrian have no influence on the light. The light does not turn from red to green simply because we want it to or ask it to.

Other people urge us to believe that *prayer can do everything.* Absolutely nothing is beyond the power of prayer. It makes no difference how bad the problem, how complicated the situation, how impossible the task, all a person needs to do is pray. The remedy is always the same: pray about it.

Such people recognize that the universe is not so inflexible, and behind it all is the Creator who has power over the laws He has established. Yet, the Christian must guard against the concept that prayer is a magic formula by which we manipulate God into doing things for us. Prayer is not a magic formula by which a person can make God jump through hoops. God is not a divine vending machine responding automatically to our desires.

The mature Christian approach lies between these two views. This approach affirms that *prayer does make a difference!* It recognizes that there is someone in the universe who responds to earnest prayers. This view takes seriously the biblical promises concerning prayer. At the same time, it rejects the idea that prayer is magical or that God can be manipulated.

We know for certain that prayer brings God and the one who prays closer together. Human conversation makes it possible for us to get to know one another better. We get better acquainted with God by talking with Him.

We also know that prayer can cause to happen things that otherwise might not come to pass. God is not a prisoner in the world He has created. Thinking that God's will is fixed and inflexible is a serious mistake. God responds to our prayers as a Person—not as a machine.

Prayer is not an attempt to force God to do our will; instead it is an effort to be open to His will for us. Prayer is not laying out our stubborn will before God and begging for His stamp of approval; but it is yielding our "want to" for Him to mold, alter, or reject to become the same as His will. Prayer is not telling God what to do; it is telling Him what we think we need. Prayer is not our effort to change the will of God; rather it is our effort to promote it.

Why Pray at All?

Ed seemed a little uncertain about expressing his true feelings. Finally he came out with what was really bothering him: "If God already knows what we want and need, why tell Him? Won't He just give it to us without our having to run to Him about every little thing?" There is hardly any Christian alive who has not struggled with that question. The problem is genuine and certainly not easily solved. "Why pray at all?"

TruthSearch 40

Write an answer to Ed's question.

Dear Ed:

My answer to the question Why pray at all? will be more a personal testimony than an organized explanation. I am happy to report that, after many years of theological education and more than twenty years in the ministry, I still pray. In fact, I find prayer more necessary as the years go by. I would be the first, however, to admit that I do not fully understand what happens in prayer. I do not pray because I can give a logical explanation for it. Neither do I pray because I have all the questions answered and all the problems solved.

"Then why do you pray?" you may ask.

I gladly answer. I make prayer a vital part of my personal Christian life for three basic reasons.

First of all, I pray *because God is real to me.* God is a Person. He made me a person—not a puppet. A person's highest capacity is to communicate with his Creator. I pray because God is a real person and my relationship with Him is a personal one.

Why go to God with every little concern? Because our relationship is a personal one. Even the human parent wants the child to open up his heart without fear, though most of what is told is already known. Does this mean that family conversation is useless? Of course not! The thoughtful husband expresses his love for his wife in spite of the fact that she already knows he loves her. Why? Because such expressions are part of what it means to live on a truly personal level. Our prayers are not needed to inform God about things He does not know. They are needed as a recognition of our personal fellowship with the Father.

TruthSearch 41

How is praying like nurturing a friendship? Write your answer.

Second, I pray *because Jesus prayed and taught His followers to pray.* Have you ever thought much about the fact that Jesus prayed? Every time I struggle with the problems related to prayer, I pause and reflect on the fact that Jesus actually prayed. He is my Lord and He prayed. He prayed, not merely to set an example, but because He needed to pray. If prayer was necessary for Jesus, what about you and me?

At their request, Jesus gave His disciples some specific advice concerning prayer. Commonly called the "Lord's Prayer," it should be called the "Disciples' Prayer." Jesus said: "This . . . is how you should pray:

'Our Father in heaven:
   May your holy name be honored: as we forgive the wrongs that others have done to us.
   may your Kingdom come:
   may your will be done on earth as it is in heaven.
   Give us today the food we need. Do not bring us to hard testing, but keep us safe from the Evil One.'"
   forgive us the wrongs we have done,

—Matthew 6:9-13, GNB

Most of us have memorized this Model Prayer. Yet, Jesus never intended that it be repeated over and over until it becomes empty words. He intended that it be a guide by which you measure your own prayer life. Look at it with this idea in mind.

When you pray, do you have any trouble thinking of God as a loving, Heavenly Father? Is He understanding, forgiving, approachable? For Jesus, prayer was a conversation between Father and child. "May your holy name be honored" reveals proper reverence (v. 9).

Also, Jesus saw prayer as the way God reveals His will to us. It makes a great difference whether you pray "My will be done" or "Your will be done" (v. 10). It is the difference between a heavenly Santa Claus and a Heavenly Father. Prayer is letting God get through to you to teach you His will. The ultimate aim is for every person to be personally committed to God's will.

God wants us to tell Him what our needs are (v. 11). The "daily bread" request is for more than literal bread. It is a request for all the needs that sustain life. You need more than bread, right? Tell God what you think you need.

Prayer is also a request for forgiveness and the practice of forgiving (v. 12). Each of us needs forgiveness. Why? Because "all have sinned and fall short of the glory of God" (Rom. 3:23). Many people accumulate much guilt over sins in their lives. What should they do about it? Get rid of it! In prayer ask for God's forgiveness and cleansing. Then say, "Thank you, Lord, for doing what you promised."

But watch that cliff-hanger, "as we forgive the wrongs that others have done to us" (v. 12). When you pray, do you have bad feelings toward others? Do you nurse hatreds and hold grudges? God is under no obligation to forgive us as long as we have not forgiven others. Notice the verses immediately following the "Disciples' Prayer" (Model Prayer): "If you forgive others the wrongs they have done to you, your Father in heaven will also forgive you. But if you do not forgive others, then your Father will not forgive the wrongs you have done" (Matt. 6:14-15, GNB).

Finally, according to Jesus, prayer is asking God to protect us from temptations and to deliver us during times of testing (v. 13). Prayer is good preventive medicine. Sometimes it is better not even to be exposed to temptation than it is to try to resist it. This is where God and prayer come in. Most of us are like the young man who confessed, "I can resist anything but temptation." In our prayers we should ask God to direct our paths away from temptation.

Jesus saw prayer as being absolutely essential for the Christian. He prayed and taught His followers to pray. For that reason, and others, I have made prayer a habit of my life.

TruthSearch 42

Write a phrase from the Model Prayer (Matt. 6:9-13) that relates to each need:

I want everyone to know God.

_____

Why can't people live God's way?

_____

I need food but I also need friends, Lord.

_____

I made that guy feel terrible by what I said to him.

_____

But he started it!

_____

What should I do about that party, Lord?—There will be drinking.

_____

The devil seems to have so much power . . . he seems so strong.

_____

Third, I pray *because of the prayer promises* recorded in the Bible. Christ gave us bold promises about prayer. Imagine being a new Christian. You are just beginning to read your Bible for the first time. In the process you stumble onto the following prayer promises: Mark 11:24; Matthew 18:19; John 14:14; Matthew 21:22. Read those promises right now.

I am challenged by the boldness of these prayer promises. Frankly, there are times when they do not seem to agree with the facts of experience. When that happens, I do not stop praying. I probe more deeply into Christ's meaning behind these promises.

Where Do I Begin?

One evening I was speaking about prayer to a group of people. I noticed that Thomas was fidgety. His wrinkled brow told me he could hardly wait for the discussion period. I was right. He was the first to speak.

"Pastor," he began, "you assume too much. You must think we already know how to pray. I don't know about the others, but I don't know how to pray. I don't even know where to begin."

Such confession was not easy. Everybody else looked so sure and pious. But Thomas was not one to spend the rest of his life nursing unanswered questions. So, with great courage, he asked, "Where do I begin?"

The question deserves an answer. You will do well to remember that *even the simplest prayer should have three parts.* Elton Trueblood has suggested that any person has made a great beginning in prayer when he sincerely utters three brief statements: "Thank you, Lord!" "Help me!" "Help John and Mary!"[1]

Start with "Thank you, Lord" (see Phil. 4:4-7). God has given you so much! *Thanks* is one of the few things you can give Him. Begin thanking God for the things He has already done in your life. Gratitude is the healthiest emotion known to humanity.

Continue with "Help me" (see Mark 11:22-25). If you are like I am, you need all the help you can get. God cares about the things you care about. You can talk to Him about everything important to you. Invite God to share the real stuff that makes up your daily life.

Confess your sins to God. Name the things you have done wrong. Tell God that you are sorry. Ask His forgiveness. Then, believe He has done what He promised: "If we confess our sins, He is faithful . . . to forgive our sins and to cleanse us from all unrighteousness" (1 John 1:9).

Finally, concentrate on the needs of others. End your prayer with "Help John and Mary." (See Jas. 5:13-16.) You may want to make a prayer list of the names of individuals you wish to remember in prayer. Be specific. Call names before God and specify their needs. It is rewarding to watch God at work in the lives of those you love. Pray for them daily.

TruthSearch 43

PRAYER PRACTICE

THANK: Read Philippians 4:4-7. Write at least five things you want to thank God for:

1.

2.

3.

4.

5.

HELP ME: Read Mark 11:22-25. Write three requests for God's help:

1.

2.

3.

HELP THEM: Read James 5:13-16. List the names of at least five persons you want to remember in prayer. Beside each name write the need(s) of the person.

1.

2.

3.

4.

5.

One of the first rules for beginning pray-ers is *regularity*. Pray each day and, as much as possible, at the same time. Set a fixed time for private prayer even though you are attempting to carry on continual conversation with God throughout the day. Select the time best for you, and stick to it.

Matters such as time, place, form, and posture are intensely personal. The value of prayer at the beginning of the day is that God's guidance can be sought for the plans and activities of that day. We also can request God's strength for the known and unknown, the good and evil that will come to us each day.

The place of prayer should be completely private and as free as possible from interruptions. Jesus advised: "When you pray, go to your room, close the door, and pray to your Father, who is unseen. And your Father, who sees what you do in private, will reward you" (Matt. 6:6, GNB). If you can be sure that no one will see, hear, or interrupt, you will be able to concentrate better.

There is a time to pray alone (most of the time), and a time to pray with others. Jesus both participated in and encouraged praying with a group. One of His greatest promises was concerning the prayer of two: "'If two of you agree on earth about anything they may ask, it shall be done for them by My Father who is in heaven'" (Matt. 18:19).

Posture does not matter to God. It matters to us only as it reflects our attitude. Certainly all prayer cannot be expressed with heads bowed and eyes closed. You may stand, sit, kneel, or lie down to pray. The only advantage to kneeling is that it reflects an attitude of humility. Lying down may contribute more to sleepiness than concentration.

How long should you pray? As long as praying is meaningful and helpful—and no longer. I have discovered that it is more natural for me to pray regularly and briefly than it is to indulge in long, marathon prayers one day and then skip several days. Jesus said, "'When you are praying, do not use meaningless repetition, as the Gentiles do, for they suppose they will be heard for their many words'" (Matt. 6:7). Remember, Jesus' Model Prayer was only sixty-eight words long. With God, longwindedness is not a virtue.

When I Don't Feel Like Praying

"What do I do when the excitement is gone?" Ron asked. "Prayer is just words. There's nobody there."

Let's admit that the Christian life has good days and bad days. We all have our bouts with the spiritual blahs. Many people, at such times, simply stop praying altogether, which is the worst possible response. This leaves God with no point of contact. Remember, the spiritual blahs, like the common cold, are neither permanent nor fatal.

You should *continue to pray whether you feel like it or not!* Why? Because the continual Christian life is like regular eating habits. Some meals are exciting. Others are ordinary. But we are fed.

It is better to keep in contact with God and talk with Him regularly. When we pray, we can work through our problems and grow spiritually. Stay in touch with God . . . even when you don't feel like it.

Honestly Now

Building some basic spiritual disciplines into your life will enrich your relationship with God and others. Prayer is one of those basic disciplines. The totally undisciplined life is never a live option for the Christian. We are never free from certain spiritual habits. Be honest with God. Tell Him how you feel.

---

[1]D. Elton Trueblood, *A Place to Stand* (New York: Harper and Row, 1969), 100. Used by permission.

8

The Miracle of the Church

Memory Verse: *Acts 2:42* (card 13)

In this chapter, for our area of searching, we will concentrate on the nature of the

$$\overline{\epsilon\kappa\kappa\lambda\eta\sigma\acute{\iota}\alpha}$$

church

The symbol of our search will be the spire.

■■ I BELIEVE IN AND LOVE THE CHURCH. In my search for a maturing faith, I have discovered that Christ loved the church (see Eph. 5:25). This is a *truth that makes a difference.* I would like to change some things about the church; others I would like to keep. But, that doesn't disturb me.

Remember, it is possible to affirm our love for the church while we continue to seek change and to come to a better understanding of this complex organism.

The church is slow to change. It needs your prayers and understanding. It is good to remember that, even though a motorcycle can execute a U-turn quicker than a trailer truck, it's the truck that delivers the goods in the long run. In my own experience I have discovered that the church has spent more time waiting on me to change than I have spent waiting on it.

On the Outside—Looking In

What if you were asked to draw some conclusions about the church based entirely on the habits and practices of Christians?

A man from Mars was asked to write a research paper on "The Religion of America." Since he did not know the language, his conclusions were based strictly on observation. He concluded that Americans are sun worshipers.

The man from Mars listed numerous reasons for arriving at that conclusion. First, he noted that, one day each week, Americans by the thousands go to seashores and lakesides to worship. He observed that millions of dollars were spent annually for the equipment necessary for sun worship. By their dress and actions, the people revealed a complete submission to the god of the sun. From intensive research he also discovered that they met on *sun-day*.

In an attempt to be objective, the Martian felt that it was necesary to mention the existence of a peculiar sect of anti-sun worshipers. On the same day of the week they would go to buildings with stained glass windows (obviously to keep out the rays of the sun). They worshiped a little-known Jehovah God. By their dress and activities they were obviously in rebellion against the sun god. They called their meeting day "Lord's Day," in preference to sun-day.

Of course, the man's observations were superficial—just what you would expect of a man from Mars.

TruthSearch 44

If that same Martian were to observe the students in your school, what conclusions would he come to regarding their worship practices?

What Is the Church?

That's easy, you say. The church is that red brick building at the corner of Webster and Comanche. One problem. In the New Testament the word *church* is never used to refer to a building or, for that matter, to a denomination.

If you decided to destroy your church, what would you do? What weapons would you use? Would you set fire to the building? Tear out the baptistry? Burn all the budgets? No. The New Testament concept of the church had no connection with a church building.

Some people look upon the church as an institution in the community that offers certain services from time to time. It is necessary to continue official membership in the church in order to use its facilities in connection with baptism, marriage, and death. This mild form of vague religion falls far short of the New Testament concept of the church.

The word *church* literally means the "called out ones." The church is not the building; it is believers banded together to carry out Christ's orders. In the New Testament the word is used with a twofold meaning. In some instances it refers to the whole body of believers,—the fellowship of the redeemed everywhere, the people of God assembled or unassembled. In most cases, however, church refers to a local congregation.

Before ascending to the Father, the risen Christ told us what we should be busy doing as a church: "'All authority has been given to Me in heaven and on earth. Go therefore and make disciples of all the nations, baptizing them in the name of the Father and the Son and the Holy Spirit, teaching them to observe all that I commanded you; and lo, I am with you always, even to the end of the age'" (Matt. 28:18-20). The task of the church has never changed. Unfortunately, we have learned quite well how to live with the commands given in the Great Commission without doing them or feeling guilty about our disobedience.

Another favorite concept of *church* in the New Testament is fellowship. Paul, in writing to the Corinthian Church, closed his letter with the familiar benediction referring to "the fellowship of the Holy Spirit" (2 Cor. 13:14). This fellowship of loving concern was a product of the Spirit's presence.

A picture of this fellowship is recorded in the early chapters of Acts. Luke said of the three thousand newly baptized converts: "They were continually devoting themselves to the apostles' teaching, and to fellowship, to the breaking of bread and to prayer" (Acts 2:42). This was a twofold fellowship: (1) with God in the experience of worship, and (2) with fellow believers in a sharing of faith, a caring for one another's needs, and a bearing of one another's burdens.

TruthSearch 45

Memorize Acts 2:42 by listing the actions of the first-century believers:

They were continually devoting themselves

- to the _____ _____ ,
- and to _____ ,
- to the _____ of _____
- and to _____ .

When the church becomes a fellowship of loving concern, it will attract the attention of the outside world. Jesus said, "Love one another. . . By this all men will know that you are my disciples" (John 13:34-35). The most persuasive of all qualities is that of genuine love and concern. Unless people see in us the practice of love, they will not and should not listen when we speak to them of spiritual matters. A church that has become an unloving fellowship contradicts everything Christ taught us.

Would you like to become involved in a task that is of utmost importance to God? Then give your assistance in creating a fellowship of loving concern in your church. People do not rebel against the church as it is defined here. What they do rebel against is the distortion or perversion of the church as they have seen it in some unloving fellowship.

Where Is the Church on Monday?

This question presents no problem to those who go to church (meaning the building) on Sunday and give little thought to Christianity the rest of the week. For them the church is at the corner of Webster and Comanche regardless of the day of the week. But, what if the church is not the building but is the believers? What if the church is a fellowship of loving concern, whether the people are assembled or not assembled? Then the question has significance: Where is the church on Monday?

The Christian life is characterized by a rhythm of come and go. Christ's commands to His followers reveal a creative tension between invitation and commission. On one hand He invited, "'Come to Me . . . and I will give you rest'" (Matt. 11:28). On the other hand he urged, "'Go . . . and make disciples of all the nations'" (Matt. 28:19).

This come-and-go rhythm continues to point to the tension in the life of the Christian. The church is to be both gathered and scattered. There are times when we should assemble—come together; there are times when we should be scattered—go out.

On Sunday the church gathers together for the purpose of Bible study, worship, training, and prayer. These are necessary times if we wish to sustain a vital Christian experience. During these times of assembly, we come to know the Lord better; we come to a better understanding of the Christian life; and we encourage one another to be faithful. This is half the story.

Where is the church on Monday or the rest of the week? During the week the individual Christian goes out into all his world communicating the good news. Our primary ministry is not in the church but in the world.

On Monday the church is where you are—on the job, at home with your family, in your leisure hours, at school, on the athletic field, where you take an exam, or go on a date.

The creative tension of come and go is normal in the Christian life. There is no reason to fear or resent it. The tension is a necessary part of the challenge and excitement of following Christ.

Would Jesus Go to Church?

Many people wonder if Jesus would have time for today's church. Would He attend our worship? Would He identify with the life and ministry of churches today? Even more important, does the church deserve a place in our busy, hectic lives? The answer is important as you can see.

I think the answer is, "Yes." Jesus went to the Passover feast when many people thought that He wouldn't. I am convinced that Jesus would have time for today's church. We simply cannot enlist Him as one who would minimize the value of the church.

What would be Jesus' attitude toward this institution? Is it possible that He would work from within to bring renewal and restoration? Because He loved the church and gave Himself for it, doesn't it make sense to think that He would keep fighting for the church to mean something. I believe that Jesus would work for meaningful change within the church while stating that, outside the church, there is little good news.

Would Jesus be able to put up with all the hypocrites in the church? He did when he lived on earth. As sensitive as he was to hypocrisy, He went to the synagogue on the Sabbath—"as His custom was." Where will we go to escape hypocrites?

A hypocrite is a pretender or play-actor. Such a person is not trying and failing. He is failing to try. This works two ways. If it is hypocritical to come to church and pretend to be something you're not, isn't it just as hypocritical to stay outside and pretend that you don't need the church, when you really do? We come to church, not because we are good, but because we are not and know we ought to be.

Would Jesus be satisfied with the negative views of some church members? He wasn't satisfied with such attitudes before. He worked to change the legalistic, negative approach of the Pharisees. He refused to believe that people could be forced to enjoy God by forbidding them to enjoy anything else.

Jesus' entire ministry was given to show that Christianity was more than a list of "Thou shalt not's." He stated openly that His followers' brand of religion would have to be better than that of the Pharisees. He turned religious commitment toward the positive when He said, "'You shall love the Lord your God with all your heart, and with all your soul, and with all your mind, and with all your strength. . . . You shall love your neighbor as yourself'" (Mark 12:30-31). Jesus insisted that these are the greatest commandments.

TruthSearch 46

What do you think Jesus would like least about your church? Why?

What do you think He would like most? Why?

What About You and Your Church?

You knew this question would come up sooner or later. Does the church deserve a place in *your* busy, hectic life? Will you have time for today's church? Will you attend its worship services? Will you identify with its life and ministry?

Many people have mixed feelings about the church. Before you definitely decide that the church is wrong, consider the following truths: (1) Jesus encouraged setting aside a day primarily for worship, fellowship, and rest. (2) He saw the sabbath—a day of worship—as one of God's good gifts to make life fuller and better for people. (3) He said to the religious leaders of His day, "'The Sabbath was made for man, and not man for the Sabbath'" (Mark 2:27). In this overly active, restless, nerve-shattering age, people need the calm, poise-restoring influence of a day of worship.

Jesus resented the inhumanity, intolerance, and rules religion of the Pharisees who turned the day of worship into a burden rather than a blessing. He urged His disciples not to follow their example: "Do not . . . imitate their actions, because they don't practice what they preach. They tie onto people's back loads that are heavy and hard to carry, yet they aren't willing even to lift a finger to help them carry those loads" (Matt. 23:3-4, GNB).

As Christians we must remember that He whom we call Lord of life is also Lord of the sabbath: "For the Son of Man is Lord of the Sabbath" (Matt. 12:8). Jesus respected the sabbath and made it a practice to attend public worship: "He came to Nazareth, where He had been brought up; and as was His custom, He entered the synagogue on the Sabbath" (Luke 4:16). If Jesus is Lord of our lives and Lord of the sabbath, we are directly responsible to Him for how we use the day of worship.

Why did Jesus form a habit of regular attendance at public worship? After all, wasn't Nazareth a small town with ordinary people? The synagogue was a little place with worship services that probably were not particularly inspiring. The hypocrites and Pharisees were there. Legalism and negative attitudes were as thick as peanut butter. If Jesus didn't agree with much that was going on, why did He keep going?

Could it be that Jesus knew the value of a time, place, and associations that make the presence of God more sure? You may ask, "But, can't we worship God anywhere?" Yes, but most of the time we don't. Most of us need the encouragement of a fellowship of loving concern, a fellowship where fires are rekindled, courage is regained, and temptations are conquered.

TruthSearch 47

Draw a picture or write a sentence describing something your church does to encourage you to live your faith.

Draw a picture or write a sentence describing what you do or say that encourages others in your church to live their faith.

Could it be that Jesus saw in the church a potential militant army marching off the map with the good news about His kingdom? If not the church, then who?

Jesus lived and died believing that ultimate victory was with the church. After Peter confessed his belief that Jesus was the Messiah, Jesus said: "You are Peter, and upon this rock I will build My church; and the gates of Hades shall not overpower it" (Matt. 16:18).

I am aware of the weaknesses and failures of the church. Actually the basic problem is largely personal and spiritual. Part of the maturing process is accepting responsibility for our own failures. Perhaps it is time for you and me to admit that we are partly to blame for the poor showing of the church. The church's failure is our failure.

With all its faults and shortcomings, the church remains the Body of Christ. Because of one bad experience, some people write off the church. When this happens, they are doing the cause of Christ and themselves a great injustice. That would be like giving up baths because one time you got into a tub and the water was too hot or too cold. It is best to keep working at it until you get the water just right.

I urge you to stay with the church. Keep fighting and praying for the church to mean something. Help bring about the necessary changes. Instead of kicking on the outside, work on the inside.

A close relationship to the church will help you avoid two extremes: an isolation from the world that would result in a "holier-than-thou" attitude and an imitation of the world that would result in a "worldier-than-thou" attitude.

Why Do We Need the Church?

The church is not optional for the believer. It is essential for vital Christianity.

We need the church, first of all, because *it constantly confronts the non-Christian world with the claims of Christ.* As noted earlier in this chapter, the risen Christ commissioned His church to do three things: (1) make disciples in all nations, (2) baptize them, and (3) teach them to obey all His commands (see Matt. 28:19-20). The work of the church is not complete until these three important matters are accomplished for every person. The church is uniquely qualified to carry out this Commission—not in part but in full.

TruthSearch 48

Write your first name vertically in the boxed area below. Then read Matthew 28:18-20. Beginning with each letter of your name, write one way you could help accomplish the purposes of the church through your own local church.

Over the years many small groups have developed outside the church, competing for the attention of Christians. It is not a question of whether these groups are good or bad. Some people are blessed by these small groups during some critical years of their Christian experience.

Before a person allows such groups to become substitutes for the church, he should ask some further questions: Is this group carrying out the Great Commission of Christ: Is this group interested in training the new convert as well as winning that person to Christ? Will this group minister to my spiritual needs the rest of my life, or is it limited to a few years? Is this group interested in baptizing the new convert as Christ commanded? If any of these questions receive a negative answer, the group will never be a worthy substitute for the church.

We also need the church because *it provides the fellowship and resources necessary for Christian growth.* You and I need all the help we can get to live the Christian life. In the church we keep an eye on one another. We watch after one another. We encourage one another in the improvement of our weaknesses. We praise one another because of our strengths. We stimulate one another to noble living. We provide a fellowship of acceptance that gives even the outsider a sense of belonging. This is the church at its best.

The Book of Acts contains a beautiful glimpse of the ministry of the early church. On Paul's first missionary journey, stones were hurled at him outside the city of Lystra, and he was left for dead: "While the disciples stood around him, he arose and entered the city" (Acts 14:20). Some people had done what they could to silence Paul. They walked away satisfied with a job well-done. Then the disciples came and formed a circle around him. They nursed his wounds. They gave him strength and encouragement. They put fresh heart and determination into him. Finally, on his own strength, he went back into the same city. The ministry of the church is to form a circle of love and concern around all believers in their times of need.

As Christians, we need one another. We need the strength, comfort, encouragement, and stimulation to noble living that comes from the fellowship of the church. The writer of Hebrews issued a challenge and a warning to every believer: "Let us consider how to stimulate one another to love and good deeds, not forsaking our own assembling together, as is

the habit of some, but encouraging one another; and all the more, as you see the day drawing near" (Heb. 10:24-25).

The writing of the New Testament was not complete; yet some believers had already formed the habit of neglecting public worship. William Barclay warned, "There is no man who can live the Christian life and neglect the fellowship of the Church."[2] You may disagree with this statement. I have watched many Christians attempt to disprove it. Most of them became hopelessly cold and indifferent to spiritual things.

There is no more effective denial of all Christ means than to remove oneself from the fellowship of believers. Generally, when the Christian neglects worship, spiritual growth stops. That person begins to live for trifles, and the light of hope leaves his eyes.

Finally, we need the church because *it is the most effective protection against going back to old ways.* A constant possibility facing every Christian is that his heart will turn away from God and back to those things that were part of his life before he became a Christian. When this happens, the major results will be spiritual loneliness and neglect of spiritual resources.

We need the mutual encouragement we receive within the fellowship of the church: "Encourage one another day after day, as long as it is still called 'Today,' lest any one of you be hardened by the deceitfulness of sin" (Heb. 3:13). The fellowship of mutual encouragement is a priceless treasure.

TruthSearch 49

Read Hebrews 3:13. Write three actions you could take to encourage another youth who is a member of your church.

1.

2.

3.

The Miracle of the Church

It looks as though the church is here to stay. If the church were going to be destroyed by external criticism or to commit suicide by indifference within, it would have happened long ago. You and I are confronted constantly with the miracle of the church.

Periodically, I visit with people who have either given up on the church or consider that God has passed it by. They seem to feel sorry for me, because my life is committed to an institution that is on the way out. Then I remember the words of Jesus: "Upon this rock I will build My church; and the gates of Hades shall not overpower it" (Matt. 16:18). I begin to look around at other possibilities. Is there an organization outside the church that has the stamp of God's approval? Has God provided us a substitute for the church? When I compare the outside possibilities to what the church could be if it really came alive, my decision is to stay with the church and work for its renewal.

The church has survived the neglect and indifference of many of its members. Nothing but a divine institution under the direct blessing of God could have survived the shallow, superficial commitment of so many people. The miracle of the church is that it survives!

The church not only survives, it also contains the greatest number of people committed to God to be found anywhere. Where else would you go to find a greater number of potential recruits for what God wishes to do in today's world?

I urge you to stay close to the church. That's where the action is! What happens to and in the church is supremely important in today's world. And, what happens in the world will depend largely on what first happens in your church.

The greatest miracle of all is that the church is open to all kinds of people. The church is more a "sinners' anonymous" than a "saints' conservatory." We must never forget that "Whosoever will may come."

Honestly Now

What kind of church member are you? List some ways in which your church could be improved. Beside each item, write how you can help your church to be better in each area.

Improvements Needed	Ways I Can Help

[1] From *The Encyclopedia of Religious Quotations*, edited and compiled by Frank S. Mead (Old Tappan, New Jersey: Fleming H. Revell Company, 1965), 75. Used by permission.

[2] William Barclay, *The Letter to the Hebrews* (Philadelphia: The Westminster Press, 1955), 137.

[3] Mead, *op. cit.*, 75.

9

The Ordinances: Baptism and the Lord's Supper

Memory Verses: *Romans 6:4; 1 Corinthians 11:26* (cards 14-15)

Thousands of years from now when archaeologists uncover a Baptist church, regardless of its size or geographical location, they will find that two things occupied places of importance. One will be a modern convenience called a baptistry—a watertight tank large enough for complete immersion. The other will be a table, located front and center, from which the Lord's Supper was served, with the words *In Remembrance of Me* inscribed on it.

The New Testament church had two ordinances: baptism and the Lord's Supper. These two observances form a backdrop for a symbolic drama of Christianity. The drama has two acts. Each act reveals things to remember about the life, ministry, death, and resurrection of Jesus Christ.

The purpose of this chapter is to explore the meaning of

βαπτίζω   and   κυριακὸν δεῖπνον

baptism   Lord's Supper

The cup and bread will serve as our symbol.

■■ I BELIEVE BAPTISM AND THE LORD'S SUPPER ARE SYMBOLIC ACTS THAT JESUS COMMANDED US TO OBSERVE. These observances picture what Jesus did to make our salvation possible (see Matt. 28:19; Luke 22:19; 1 Cor. 11:23-26). They clearly symbolize *truths that make a difference.*

Remember, it is possible to affirm the fact that every believer should be baptized and should participate in the observance of the Lord's Supper while we search for deeper understanding of these observances.

The word *ordinance* means "a decree or command." Baptists use the word to refer to the two observances ordained by Christ: Baptism and the Lord's Supper. In order to understand why we as Baptists observe these church ordinances, we must interpret them in the light of the New Testament teachings they symbolize.

The Ordinance of Baptism

"Why all the fuss about baptism?" Mike wanted to know. "Haven't I heard you say that baptism isn't necessary to salvation? If baptism doesn't help save us, then why is so much emphasis placed on being baptized when a person wants to join the church?" Many young people struggle with this question.

TruthSearch 50

Write an answer to Mike's question. Feel free to refer to the material that follows for help in writing your answer.

The answer to Mike's question is in chronology—the order in which things happen. Two questions are important: (1) How does an individual become a Christian? (2) What should a person do after he or she becomes a Christian? Baptism comes into the picture only when we discuss the second question.

Baptism does not save. Nor does it complete one's salvation. Still, every believer must take baptism seriously for three reasons: (1) because Jesus Himself was baptized, (2) because Jesus placed His stamp of approval on the baptismal activity of His disciples, and (3) because Jesus commissioned His followers to baptize new converts.

The Scriptures record Jesus' desire to be baptized: "Then Jesus arrived from Galilee at the Jordan coming to John, to be baptized by him" (Matt. 3:13).

"But John tried to prevent Him, saying, 'I have need to be baptized by You,'" (Matt. 3:14).

But Jesus said, "'Permit it at this time; for in this way it is fitting for us to fulfill all righteousness.' Then he permitted Him'" (Matt. 3:15).

By submitting to John's baptism, Jesus placed His stamp of approval on John's ministry, set an example for all His followers, and dedicated Himself publicly to a redemptive ministry. In baptism He symbolized His death, burial, and resurrection.

In John 4:1-2, we read of a time when more people were coming to Jesus to be baptized than to John. A note of explanation was added: "Jesus Himself was not baptizing, but His disciples were." Apparently Jesus agreed to this practice of baptism.

At the close of His physical ministry on earth, the risen Christ gave His "marching orders" to the New Testament church. His instructions were to go and make disciples of all nations, "'baptizing them in the name of the Father and the Son and the Holy Spirit'" (Matt. 28:19).

What Is the Purpose of Baptism?

Because baptism is symbolic in nature and not sacramental (does not impart grace), the next consideration must be its purpose or meaning. What does baptism symbolize? What are the "things worth remembering" that are constantly called to mind by this symbolic drama?

First of all, baptism points back in time to the death, burial, and resurrection of Jesus. Each baptism is a picture of these central affirmations of the Christian faith. Baptism symbolizes a salvation that comes by faith in Christ.

A second purpose of baptism is to dramatize the present experience of the believer. Baptism symbolizes or pictures death to sin, burial with Christ, and resurrection to walk a new life with Him. Paul described it beautifully: "Therefore we have been buried with Him through baptism into death, in order that as Christ was raised from the dead through the glory of the Father, so we too might walk in newness of life" (Rom. 6:4).

"...and raised to walk in a completely new life with Christ."

Baptism is a part of the new convert's public testimony of faith in Christ. When the believer walks down into the baptismal waters, he is saying, "I have died to an old, sinful way of life." When he is placed beneath the water, he is saying, "I am being buried to the old way of life." Then, as he is raised out of the water, he is saying, "I am being raised to walk in a completely new life with Christ."

Baptism, then, is an outward symbol of an inward experience. Unless the person being baptized has already had the inner, rebirth experience, baptism is robbed of its meaning. For that reason, throughout their history, Baptists have baptized believers only.

In this respect, baptism may be compared to a marriage ceremony. Taking marriage vows does not *cause* two people to fall in love. The wedding ceremony is assumed to be an outward sign or symbol of an inner love and commitment that already exists.

TruthSearch 51

Pretend you are talking to someone who knows nothing about baptism. Describe what baptism symbolizes:

What Should Be the Mode of Baptism?

Baptists did not choose their name. In the sixteenth century a group of Christians insisted that only believers should be baptized, but they did not insist on immersion as the mode or method of baptizing. This group was given the name "Anabaptists" (rebaptizers). In the seventeenth century, when a group of Christians began to teach that only believers should be baptized and that the mode should be immersion, they were branded Anabaptists. In an effort to shun that name, this group of Christians began calling themselves "Baptized churches" or "Churches of the Baptized Way." By the middle of the seventeenth century, opponents began using the name "Baptists," and some Baptists also began using the name. Toward the eighteenth century, *Baptists* was the generally accepted title.

As you might expect, the people called *Baptists* had some strong convictions about baptism. Two of these convictions emerged early and remain at the heart of Baptist teachings: (1) insistence upon the baptism of believers only, and (2) baptism by immersion only. Our present concern is with the second conviction—that immersion constitutes the act of baptism.

Why do Baptists continue to insist upon immersion? Isn't it true that many church groups now use sprinkling and pouring as methods of baptizing? Aren't these methods less expensive and more convenient? The answer to the last two questions is yes. Now, let me attempt to answer the first question. Basically there are three reasons why Baptists have continued to practice immersion.

The first reason Baptists use immersion as the method for baptism relates to the meaning of the word used for baptism in the New Testament. The Greek word *baptizo* means to "dip, plunge, submerge, or immerse." Most Christian scholars agree that the New Testament method for baptism was immersion. Classical Greek used the word *baptizo* to describe a ship sinking into the sea.

A second reason for the insistence on immersion is that descriptions of baptism in the New Testament suggest immersion. The Gospel of Mark carries this account of the baptism of Jesus by John in the Jordan River: "Immediately coming up out of the water, He saw the heavens opening" (1:10). In addition, the record of Philip baptizing the eunuch presents a clear description of immersion: "They both went down into the water, . . . and he baptized him. And when they came up out of the water, the Spirit of the Lord snatched Philip away; and the eunuch saw him no more, but went on his way rejoicing" (Acts 8:38-39).

The final reason Baptists insist on immersion is a logical one that relates to the meaning of the symbolism. What is baptism intended to symbolize? We already have concluded that it symbolizes death, burial, and resurrection (see Rom. 6:2-4). Only immersion fully accomplishes this symbolism.

Generally it is agreed that immersion was the original form of baptism. Baptists have felt that it is impossible to change the mode without changing the meaning. For that reason we have continued to immerse those who come for membership in our churches.

TruthSearch 52

Complete the following sentences to state the three reasons Baptists insist on immersion as the method for baptism:

1. *Baptizo,* the Greek word for "baptize" means _____ .

2. _____ of baptism in the New Testament suggest immersion.

3. Baptism symbolizes _____ ,

_____ , and _____ .
Only immersion can picture these truths.

If you could not complete the sentences, read again the previous section to find the answers.

Who Should Be Baptized?

Do you remember how we got our name? We are called *Baptists* because we have some strong convictions about baptism. We have already discussed one of these convictions—that baptism should be by immersion only. Now we are ready to examine another conviction—our insistence on the *baptism of believers only.*

As emphasized already, careful study shows that believers' baptism was the only kind of baptism practiced in New Testament times. A certain order repeated itself: (1) an individual heard the gospel, (2) accepted its message, (3) believed in Christ as personal Savior, and (4) was baptized. The chronology of the Great Commission is important: first we are to "make disciples," next we are to "baptize them," then they must be "taught" how to live the Christian life (see Matt. 28:19-20). Believers are the only proper subjects for baptism.

John the Baptist demanded actions that indicated repentance before he would baptize those who came to him. He said "'Do those things that will show that you have turned from your sins'" (Matt. 3:8, GNB). When Peter preached about Christ on the day of Pentecost, those who "had received his word were baptized" (Acts 2:41). According to the New Testament pattern, baptism is the believer's first opportunity to proclaim faith in Christ.

Again, baptism is an outward symbol of an inward experience. The inward experience is one of death and burial to an old way of life and resurrection to newness of life. Unless the person being baptized can testify to this experience, baptism is robbed of its meaning. For this reason, Baptists do not practice infant baptism. Because infants are not in the position to have a personal faith in Christ, any baptism performed in their behalf cannot express the meaning of Christian baptism.

Some people believe that a baby is born condemned and that baptism results in salvation for the infant. Others believe that the child from birth is in the Kingdom and that baptism and Christian training simply keep the child in the Kingdom. Baptists believe that the new-born infant is kept under the protective grace of God until he or she reaches an age of accountability or responsibility. At such time, the child can decide for himself to be a follower of Christ. When he is old enough to decide for himself, he is also old enough to be baptized by immersion. Then, his baptism can express the full meaning and intended symbolism.

One Other Question

What about an immersion performed by some other denomination? Is it true that some Baptist churches ask certain people to be immersed again?

You will find different practices among Baptist churches at this point. Some churches receive for membership persons with such baptisms, while others do not. Each congregation is autonomous (self-governing— not told what to do by any other group or any other person). A local congregation is free to decide and is also responsible for its decisions. Those who accept these baptisms generally do so only after careful study to be sure that the proper motive, meaning, purpose, and symbolism have been preserved.

Those who reject such baptisms do so for a variety of reasons. A person's baptism generally is not accepted when it was performed for its sacramental value (immersion *for* salvation). Also, a baptism might be rejected—even when immersion was the method—if it was performed by a group that does not stress believers' baptism.

When a second immersion is requested, it is generally to accomplish one or all of three things: (1) Because Baptists believe that baptism is a part of a person's public profession of faith, at times we may ask that this confession be made before a new body of baptized believers. (2) We may ask that a person's baptism show a willing commitment to a new body of beliefs. (3) We desire that all who come into membership in Baptist churches do so out of serious commitment and conviction.

TruthSearch 53

Would you like to work on some truths that are hard to understand? Read Acts 19:1-5. Answer the following questions.

What do you think is the difference between John's baptism and Christian baptism?

Is a second immersion ever necessary? If so, under what circumstances?

The Ordinance of the Lord's Supper

The second act in the church's "symbolic drama" of Christianity is the Lord's Supper. Its purpose is to reveal some "things worth remembering" about the death of Christ for a world's sin. The Lord's Supper is a powerful aid to Christian memory, because it adds sight and taste to hearing.

The observance of the Lord's Supper was instituted at the end of Jesus' earthly ministry. He and His disciples had gathered in Jerusalem to share the Passover feast. Jesus knew that this would be their last meal together. What could He say or do on this occasion to leave His followers a continuing reminder of His love and willing sacrifice? He invited them to share in a memorial supper (see Matt. 26:26-30). Unfortunately, this ordinance has been the subject of much controversy regarding its meaning and its observance.

The Four Historic Views.—Christian history reveals the following four distinct views concerning the meaning of the Lord's Supper. The first view is identified with the Catholic church and the second with the Lutheran denomination. Two men who were leaders during the reformation—John Calvin and Ulrich Zwingli—gave their names to the other two views.

1. *Roman Catholics* believe that, when the priest consecrates the bread and wine, these elements are actually changed into the substance of the flesh and blood of Christ *(transubstantiation)*. Although the appearance and taste remain the same, those who partake are eating the flesh and drinking the blood of Christ.

2. *Lutherans* deny the change of substance in the elements while affirming that Christ is bodily present "in, with, and under" the substance of bread and wine *(consubstantiation)*. Martin Luther insisted on a literal interpretation of the words "This is my body" and "This is my blood."

3. *Calvinistic* theology insists that Christ is not bodily present but is spiritually present in the elements of bread and wine. This spiritual presence, however, is different from any other spiritual presence of Jesus. In other words, a definite spiritual blessing (grace) comes to the believer in the observance of the Lord's Supper—a grace that is not available otherwise.

4. The Lord's Supper has a *symbolic meaning (Zwinglian)*. According to this view, this beautiful ordinance is strictly a memorial supper. The bread and the fruit of the vine are symbols of the broken body and spilled blood of Jesus.

The first three views have one thing in common; each teaches that participation in the observance of the Lord's Supper is a means of receiving grace. In other words, taking the elements contributes to an individual's salvation. Persons who hold these views believe that blessings come to the believer during the Lord's Supper that can be received through no other experience.

Historically, Baptists have been identified with the fourth view. Baptists believe that, when Jesus said, "This is my body," and, "This is my blood," He was speaking symbolically. He was saying that the bread and the fruit of the vine represent, picture, or symbolize His body and blood. They become visual aids portraying what Jesus did to make salvation possible for all who believe in Him.

Does this mean that Baptists deny the spiritual presence of Christ in the Lord's Supper? Not at all. We believe that His presence here is not different from His constant presence in the life of every believer or His presence in any other place in the universe. Do Baptists deny that the Lord's Supper can be a special blessing for the believer? Certainly not. What we deny is that grace is given—that a person is "more a Christian" for having participated.

TruthSearch 54

Match the terms to their description.

_____ 1. TRANSUBSTANTIATION

a. Bread and wine are symbols of Jesus' body and blood

_____ 2. CONSUBSTANTIATION

b. Bread and wine become Jesus' body and blood.

_____ 3. CALVINISTIC VIEW

c. Jesus is bodily present in bread and wine.

_____ 4. SYMBOLIC VIEW

d. Jesus is spiritually present in bread and wine.

Now circle what Baptists believe about the Lord's Supper.

What Is the Meaning of the Lord's Supper?

Because the Lord's Supper is symbolic in its significance, the main emphasis for the believer is that of a memorial. This means it is a reminder of what Jesus did for us.

To make the most of the observance requires preparation and personal effort. Many Christians have discovered new meaning in the Lord's Supper by considering the various dimensions of its message.

Jesus instituted the Supper to preserve for all future Christians an authentic memory of His sufferings. This is *the backward look* of the Supper (1 Cor. 11:26). It receives its meaning from the past. Apart from the past deed—Christ's death on the cross—the present memorial would be emptied of its meaning. While observing the Lord's Supper, remember "I have been died for, and by the Son of God, at that!"

The Lord's Supper also provides an excellent opportunity for *an inward look*. Paul admonished, "Let a man examine himself and so let him eat of the bread, and drink of the cup" (1 Cor. 11:28). Celebration and confession go well together.

In the Lord's Supper observance, the believer *looks forward* with hope: "As often as you eat this bread and drink the cup, you proclaim the Lord's death until He comes" (1 Cor. 11:26). We gain assurance from the promise of Christ's return and the knowlege that He is the ultimate Victor.

The Lord's Supper is an ordinance of the church. Its meaning, therefore, would be incomplete without *the outward look.* We not only enjoy communion with Christ but also experience communion with one another as believers. This communion is a constant reminder that we are not alone but are a part of a larger body of believers who are also trying to grow toward maturity in the Christian faith.

TruthSearch 55

Think about the last time you participated in the Lord's Supper or think about Jesus' sacrifice for you. What comes to mind when you:

Look backward—

Look inward—

Look forward—

Look outward—

Who Should Participate?

Because the Lord's Supper is a church ordinance, the church must accept the responsibility for its administration. For example, the individual church determines how often the Supper is observed. The New Testament does not contain specific instructions about how often to observe this ordinance. Paul's only advice was that, as often as we do observe it, it should be done in remembrance of Christ (1 Cor. 11:25). The same is true in discussing who should participate. Every denomination and each church has its own set of qualifications and restrictions.

Among all Christian groups there is general agreement that some restrictions are necessary. The invitation to the Lord's Table is not to all the world. Certainly it should be limited to Christians; otherwise it would lose its significance. There would be no meaning in inviting non-Christians to an observance celebrating the event that founded Christianity. The question is, How restricted should it be?

Historically, an impressive number of Baptist churches have practiced what is called "closed communion." This view holds that a person should be a member of the church in which he partakes of the Supper. The idea here is that the participant should be in the fellowship and under the discipline of the church that offers the Supper.

Many Baptist churches, however, agree that any member of any Baptist church is eligible to participate in the observance. The person would not have to be a member of the church in which he partakes of the Supper. Some Baptist churches open participation in the Supper to all believers who have been baptized according to the New Testament pattern of immersion. These churches would not require membership in a Baptist church before participation in the Supper.

Again, each congregation is an autonomous or self-governing unit. You will find different practices among Baptist churches. The final decision must be made by the church. Regardless of the view, the Lord's Supper should be presented in a loving and worshipful manner.

Honestly Now

Why did Jesus institute these ordinances? Because the heart of the gospel is set forth in their observance. They are sermons in symbols. Baptism reminds us of the death, burial, and resurrection of Jesus. It is an initial act, administered at the beginning of the Christian experience. The Lord's Supper helps us remember the sacrifice of Jesus on the cross. It is a continuing reminder, observed throughout the Christian's life.

The next time you watch someone being baptized or participate in the observance of the Lord's Supper, think deeply about the meaning of these ordinances.

10
First Things About Last Things—a Theology of Christian Hope

Memory Verse: *John 14:3* (card 16)

At one time or another, most people wonder about the future of the world. Generally, people fit into one of three groups in regard to this subject: (1) those who are so concerned with the present that they seldom think about the future, (2) those who seldom think about anything else, and (3) those who are prepared to face their deaths and are content to leave the time and details to God.

The study of the end of the world we call eschatology (*eschatos* means "last," and *logos* means "word" or "doctrine"). This chapter will present the teachings about "last things."

$$\frac{\check{\epsilon}\sigma\chi\alpha\tauο\varsigma + \lambda ο\gamma ό\varsigma}{\textbf{eschatology}}$$

No one symbol for our search is adequate. Perhaps this cluster of symbols will have meaning for you as you proceed.

■■ Before we move on, though, I want to make an affirmation: I BELIEVE THAT JESUS WILL RETURN TO EARTH. This is a truth *that makes a tremendous difference* in my life. I do not know all the details about His second coming, but that does not disturb me.

Remember, it is possible to affirm some truths while we search for greater understanding of others.

The Kingdom of God

Concern about the future of the world may be caused by a deepening pessimism about world conditions. When one views the world as sitting on a powder keg and inhabited by madmen with hands full of matches, that person has little hope.

Where is our hope? Is the human drama moving toward the final scene? Is history going somewhere or nowhere? Will goodness or nothingness prevail? What do *you* think about the future.

The study of last things is best understood as a part of the overall kingdom of God. The Kingdom had a *beginning.* Jesus began it when He came and established the rule of God in the hearts of people.

The Kingdom also *is a continuing process.* The work Jesus began continues as a spiritual experience and a present reality. Paul wrote, "I am sure that he who began a good work in you will bring it to completion at the day of Jesus Christ (Phil. 1:6, RSV).

The *final stage* of the Kingdom is the eternal kingdom to be ushered in at the second coming of Christ. God will not leave unfinished what He has begun. In His first coming He made the "down payment"; He will come again to claim those who are His.

As Christians, we believe this world had a definite beginning, and in the purpose of God, it is moving toward a fitting conclusion. In His own time, the Author of the drama will come down to the earth's stage and will announce to humanity, "Ladies and Gentlemen, it's closing time."

Should We Fear Death?

Fear of death is not unusual, even among Christians. We tend to fear anything that is unknown. At best, death remains a mystery. For most people it is a crisis that involves both major and minor changes. Most of us would prefer to be silent about death. Yet, as Christians, the least we can do is face the fact that death is a reality.

The Bible takes death seriously. In the Old Testament, death and the future life are generally presented in dark and gloomy terms. Even though death is not regarded as the "end of it all," the Old Testament does not give much light on life beyond the grave. Death is referred to as the "king of terrors" (Job 18:14).

The New Testament speaks of death as both physical and spiritual. Physical death implies being separated from the world of living persons. Spiritual death is separation from God and is described as being "dead in trespasses and sins" (see Eph. 2:1; Col. 2:13). The mystery of death is intensified when we realize that a person might be dead spiritually while still alive physically—and a person may continue to live spiritually after dying physically.

The New Testament completely transforms the concept of death. The Old Testament darkness and gloom become light and hope. Jesus referred to death as sleep (Mark 5:39), and said, "'Everyone who lives and believes in Me shall never die'" (John 11:26). His own resurrection from the dead transformed our concept of death. We cherish His promise: "'Because I live, you shall live also'" (John 14:19). This makes possible Paul's triumphant shout of faith, "For to me, to live is Christ, and to die is gain" (Phil. 1:21).

What is the Christian view of death? For the Christian death is not a dead-end street; it is a thoroughfare. Death is not the end of the drama; it is the end of the first act. Death is not a termination point; it is a gateway into eternal life. Death is understood fully only in the light of resurrection. The other side of the cross is an empty tomb. "To be continued" might well be written on every gravestone.

TruthSearch 56

Jot down—

Your feelings about death:

Your hopes about life after death:

How Jesus' resurrection affects your feelings about death:

What Does Resurrection Mean?

Job asked, "'If a man dies, will he live again?'" (Job 14:14). The clearest answer to that question was given by Jesus when He affirmed the fact of the resurrection (see Matt. 8:11; 22:23-33).

Jesus' faith in the resurrection was grounded in what He believed about the nature of God. He said, "He is not the God of the dead, but of the living" (Mark 12:27). God is not only the God of the living, but He is also the Living God. He is the God of today and the God of tomorrow. He is the God of what is and what is yet to be.

As Jesus approached the time of His own death, He talked with Martha of Bethany, one of His closest friends. He shared with her an affirmation that has become central to the Christian faith: "'I am the resurrection and the life; he who believes in Me shall live even if he dies, and everyone who lives and believes in Me shall never die'" (John 11:25-26).

As Christians we believe that the dead shall be raised. The word translated resurrection *(anastasis)* means "a raising up" or "to stand again." It refers to something dead that is made to live again. For believers in Christ, the grave is not the end. Life is more than defeat by death. We believe in resurrection because we believe that Christ was raised from the dead. Take the resurrection hope from Christianity, and you leave the gospel without listeners.

What will this new life be like? Paul sought for an illustration to help us see that the new life would be similar, yet different from the old (see

1 Cor. 15:1-58). He wrote to the Corinthians about the seed that is put in the ground and out of it grows a plant. The plant is not the same as the seed, yet it contains the same life that was in the seed. In the same way, the physical body is returned to the earth, and out of the old body comes a new one—a spiritual body—with higher powers, and yet it is continuous with the old (see 1 Cor. 15:42-49). Paul confessed that this transformation is "a great mystery" (1 Cor. 15:51). Yet, it remains the Christian's foundation of faith and hope.

First Things About the Second Coming

Jesus is coming again. We have the assurance that He will not leave unfinished what He has begun. The concept that Christ will make one final appearance at the end of the world "fits in" with the biblical perspective concerning history (Matt. 25:31; Titus 2:13). A vital part of our Christian hope is our belief in a divine event toward which the whole creation moves.

This expected appearance of Christ is called "the second coming." The New Testament word used to describe it is *parousia*, and means "presence" or "advent." Care must be taken to avoid two extremes regarding the second coming: (1) ignore it, hoping it will go away or (2) overemphasize it, giving attention to details known only to God.

My purpose here is to relate *what we can know* about the second coming from clear New Testament teachings. It is not the purpose of this brief work to deal with the differences in interpretation of the details.

One thing we know about the second coming is that *it is certain*. The fact of Jesus' return to the earth at the end of history is a central part of the biblical message. Christ Himself left us the promise: "'Let not your heart be troubled. . . . I go to prepare a place for you. And if I go and prepare a place for you, I will come again, and receive you to Myself; that where I am, there you may be also" (John 14:1-3).

TruthSearch 57

Memorize Jesus' promise in John 14:3 by filling in the blanks:

If I go and _____ a _____ for you, I will

_____ again, and _____you to Myself; that

_____ I am, _____you may be _____ .

Early in the Book of Acts it is recorded that Jesus ascended into the sky while witnesses stared after him: "As they were gazing intently into the sky while He was departing, behold, two men in white clothing stood beside them; and they also said, 'Men of Galilee, why do you stand looking into the sky? This Jesus, who has been taken up from you into heaven, will come in just the same way as you have watched Him go into heaven'" (Acts 1:10-11). The New Testament abounds in such promises.

We do not know when the second coming will occur. Jesus Himself did not know: "'But of that day and hour no one knows, not even the angels of heaven, nor the Son, but the Father alone'" (Matt. 24:36). He warned, "Be on the alert, for you do not know which day your Lord is coming" (Matt. 24:42). People are to be ready constantly: "For the Son of Man is coming at an hour when you do not think He will'" (Matt. 24:44). His coming will be as a thief in the night (Matt. 24:43).

These references point to the fact that Jesus' coming will be *sudden, mysterious,* and *unexpected.* Yet, few things have consumed so much Christian energy across the centuries as trying to pinpoint the actual time of His return. Sometimes, people take Jesus at His word when He promises to come again and then ignore His words about the uncertainty of the time in history.

To be curious about the future is easier than to be faithful in the present. This happened in Thessalonica less than thirty years after Jesus died. Some of the people were so caught up in the immediate return of the Lord that they quit their jobs and became idle busybodies who sat around discussing the future. Paul rebuked them and commanded them to do their work in quietness, to earn their own living, and not to be weary in well-doing (see 2 Thess. 3:10-13).

Jesus specifically has given us our responsibility concerning His return: "'Be ready!'" (Matt. 24:44). It helps to remember that Jesus has appointed us to the preparations committee—but not for deciding about time, place, and program. He calls for each of us to bring our lives into right relationship with God. Then we are to give our energies to living the kinds of lives that will prepare us to meet Him without shame.

Neither Jesus nor His inspired writers gave us a detailed and ordered account of the events related to His second coming. It is enough to know that Christ will return. We can leave the details to Him. When the conditions are right in God's judgment, that will be the time of the Lord's return.

TruthSearch 58

Complete the sentences.

The expected appearance of Jesus Christ is called the _____
_____ .

Jesus' return is _____ (John 14:1-3; Acts
1:10-11).

Jesus' return will be _____ ,
_____ , and _____(Matt.
24:42-44).

We are to _____ _____ for Jesus' return
(Matt. 24:44).

And Then Comes Judgment

Many people today find it difficult to believe that, sooner or later, they must sit at the judgment of results and consequences. Paul warned: "Do not be deceived, God is not mocked; for whatever a man sows, this he will also reap. For the one who sows to his own flesh shall from the flesh reap corruption, but the one who sows to the Spirit shall from the Spirit reap eternal life" (Gal. 6:7-8). These verses present both the law of identical harvest and the law of personal development—you reap what you sow. If the lower nature dominates, you may expect a harvest of trouble. If the higher nature dominates, you may expect an abundant life.

The principle of judgment in God's dealings with people runs all the way through history, human experience, and the Bible. Because human beings are created in the image of God and have moral freedom, they are also responsible to God. In a sermon preached on Mars' Hill, Paul warned the people of Athens: "'Having overlooked the times of ignorance, God is now declaring to men that all everywhere should repent, because He has fixed a day in which He will judge the world in righteousness'" (Acts 17:30-31). In Hebrews 9:27, the same truth has been stressed: "Inasmuch as it is appointed for men to die once and after this comes judgment."

When will judgment be? Certainly at the time God has appointed.

Other Scripture places it after the resurrection (Matt. 12:41-42) and at the time of the second coming of Christ (Matt. 24:40-42). Judgment will mark the end of our present world order and the beginning of an eternal order.

What is the purpose of the judgment? Obviously it is not to begin an investigation to determine whether an individual is saved or lost. A person has already determined that by his decision about Christ, made during his lifetime. Besides, the God of infinite wisdom needs no such court of investigation.

Judgment will bring to light each person's character and the total effect of his influence on others. Judgment does not decide or determine an individual's destiny. Character determines destiny. Judgment merely will assign a destiny in accordance with the person's character.

The judgment will bring the affairs of human history to a completion and, at that time, an eternal order will be initiated. The saved will be glorified because of their faith and rewarded according to their works. The unsaved will be condemned because of their unbelief and sentenced according to their works.

Judgment is never understood apart from humanity's responsibility to God. As Christians, we believe that we live in a world created by God. As free moral agents, we are free to choose or reject God. We are accountable, therefore, to Him for our lives. "In Him we live and move and exist" (Acts 17:28).

Becoming a Christian does not deliver us from responsibility; it increases our accountability. "To blame or to repent," that is the question. To blame others is to deny personal responsibility. To repent is to accept responsibility and move toward reconciliation.

TruthSearch 59

Read again the previous section and circle all the words that describe what the judgment will be like.

How does what you circled change the way you want to live today. List at least three things you're proud of in your life and three things you would like to change:

1.   1.

2.   2.

3.   3.

Are Heaven and Hell Real Places?

The final phase of our study of last things must introduce the subject of eternal destiny. Is there some way to outlive death? If so, what does eternity mean? Is there really a place of punishment called hell? What will heaven be like? There are too many questions and too little space to answer. Hold tight. The pace from here is breathtaking.

Heaven is God's eternal home where love is supreme. You will notice that Bible teachings about heaven are restrained. The Bible tells us all we need to know, but it may not tell us all we wish to know. We are told that, after the resurrection and judgment, the righteous will enter the eternal state called "heaven."

Jesus gave a description of heaven that satisfies most believers. He said, "'In My Father's house are many dwelling places'" (John 14:2). First of all, heaven is His Father's house or home. Jesus was going home—a place of security, a place where an individual can grow and share, and above all, a place of love. And there are many rooms in that home. Everyone will have a place. There will be no space problems.

Jesus further stated, "'I go to prepare a place for you'" (v. 2). Heaven is a prepared place for prepared people. It is a locality and not merely a state of being. Home was where Jesus was going to make ready living space for His followers.

Finally Jesus said, "'That where I am, there you may be also'" (v. 3). "Where I am" is perhaps our best description of heaven—it is where Jesus is!

Heaven will be a place of freedom from those things that make life difficult: sorrow, tears, pain, and death (Rev. 21:4). It also will be a place of rewards for faithful service (Matt. 25:14-30; Luke 19:12-27). In heaven we will enjoy perfect fellowship with Christ. It is a place where we may express endless gratitude (Rev. 5:9-12) and experience endless growth. With all hindrances removed, we shall go on growing in grace and serving with joy (Rev. 22:3).

Hell may be described as the opposite of heaven. While heaven is to be at home with God, hell is separation from God. Hell is where response to God is no longer possible, where love and fellowship with the Father are absent. Many people deny the reality of hell. Yet Jesus said more about hell than He did about heaven. To wish there were no hell does not change the reality. The Bible teaches that, after the resurrection and judgment, the wicked enter the eternal state of punishment called *hell* (Matt. 25:41).

The ideas of divine judgment and punishment for sin are inseparable. We already have established each person's accountability before God. Thus, sin and punishment also are inseparable. To say that a merciful God would not allow hell is to examine only one facet of God's nature. God is also just. If the wicked and righteous are to be treated alike, where is the justice of God? Besides, God does not send people to hell. They go there in spite of all God has done to prevent it.

The New Testament uses two different words for the English word *hell.* The first word, *Hades,* refers to the grave or the abode of the dead without respect to moral conditions (Matt. 11:23; 16:18; Luke 16:23; Rev. 1:18). The second word, *Gehenna,* actually denotes a place of punishment. It is the Greek name for the Valley of Hinnom located south and east of Jerusalem. At one time, human sacrifices were offered there (2 Kings 23:10). Later, it became Jerusalem's garbage dump. Fires burned continually to destroy the loathsome garbage of the city. The name of this local place, *Gehenna,* became the descriptive name for the place of eternal separation and punishment for those who choose not to know God (Rom. 1:28).

Heaven and hell are real places. Heaven is the eternal home of those who know Christ. Hell is the eternal abode of those who reject Him.

How to Live Before Christ's Coming

We spend most of our lives living "in the meantime"—waiting on significant events to happen. For two thousand years Christians have lived inbetween Christ's first coming and His second coming. We still face the difficult task of living in the in-between time. Our responsibility is to take the biblical teachings concerning the "last things" and apply them to the here and now.

Peter gave Christians clear instructions as to "what sort of people" they ought to be in light of the second coming (see 2 Pet. 3:11). "Therefore, beloved," he said, "since you look for these things, be diligent to be found by Him in peace, spotless and blameless" (2 Pet. 3:14).

TruthSearch 60

What do you look forward to most about the second coming of Jesus?

What do you want to say to Jesus when you first see Him?

What questions do you want to ask Him?

Honestly Now

Do you know why Jesus delays His return? He has a definite purpose: "Regard the patience of our Lord to be salvation" (2 Pet. 3:15). Peter also said, "The Lord is not slow about His promise, as some count slowness, but is patient toward you, not wishing for any to perish but for all to come to repentance" (2 Pet. 3:9).

Today, God calls Christians to lives of holiness and godliness. He calls those who are not Christians to repent and turn to Him.

TruthSearch 61

What choice have you made about your future?

☐ I have repented and turned to Jesus.

☐ I have ignored God.

☐ I have rejected Jesus.

Check the decision that most closely represents yours, and then write your feelings about it.

If you checked the second or third choice, we have good news for you. You can change your choice to the first one. Do that! You won't be disappointed. When you accept Jesus as your Lord and Savior, you find the best future and the best present. You are going to heaven because God promises in the Bible that you are (see Rom. 9:33; 10:13).

Group Learning Activities

These Group Learning Activities provide for active involvement of youth in the study of this book. The suggestions for the five one-hour sessions may be adapted to fit the specific needs of your group. Many of the personal learning activities (TruthSearch activities) have been incorporated into the group sessions.

For best results each youth leader should study carefully *Truths That Make a Difference: The Doctrines Baptists Believe,* complete the Truth-Search activities, and be prepared to guide the group activities.

Copies of the book should be ordered for all youth. Distribute the book prior to the first session. Encourage youth to bring their Bibles but have extras available for ones who forget to bring their own.

SESSION 1

The God I Want to Understand

(Chapters 1 and 2)

Background Scripture: John 1:14; 4:24; 1 John 1:5; 1 John 4:7-21; Matthew 16:16

Learning Goals: Youth will examine their own concepts about God, will gain a better understanding of God's qualities, and will discover why Jesus is the perfect revelation of God.

AGENDA

1. Share Ideas About God (10 Min.).
2. Memorize Truths (10)
3. Answer Questions About God's Love (10)
4. Examine Fish Symbol (10)
5. Spell Out Meaning of Incarnation (5)
6. Illustrate Human/Divine Concept (5)
7. Write Letters to God (10)

Before the Session

☐ Study carefully the Introduction and chapters 1 and 2 in *Truths That Make a Difference*. Complete the TruthSearch activities.

☐ Secure pencils, construction paper, pipe cleaners, paper cups.

☐ Record the words of 1 John 1:5 on poster board strips.

☐ Record the following questions on long strips of paper. Hang them from the ceiling.

• If God is a God of love, why is the world in the mess it's in?

• How can God love someone like me?

• Why does God allow evil?

• Does God <u>really</u> have a plan for <u>my</u> particular life?

• Is it possible that I can be someone of worth in God's eyes and in the eyes of others?

☐ Bring string, credit card forms, markers, and a rope.

☐ Cut out letters of the word *incarnation* from half pieces of paper.

During the Session

1. Share Ideas About God

• As youth arrive, direct them to draw or write their concept of God in TruthSearch 1. If you prefer, provide construction paper, pipe cleaners, and paper cups for them to use to shape their image of God.

Ask the youth to share what they wrote, drew, or shaped. Point out a significant insight from each youth's report.

• Explain that no word or picture can describe God but that each idea can help us understand Him better. Using TruthSearch 2, lead the youth to tell how persons and things can teach us about God.

• Call on three volunteers to read John 4:24; 1 John 1:5, and 1 John 4:8. Ask: What concepts about God do these verses teach? *(spirit, light, love).* Which is your favorite and why? For ideas, suggest that they scan the subtopics in chapter 1 entitled "God Is Spirit," "God Is Light," and "God Is Love."

2. Memorize Truths

• Direct attention to the Scripture Memory Cards in the center of *Truths That Make a Difference.* Explain that Scripture memory helps us recall and live truths about God such as the three we have just discussed (God is spirit, light, love). State that you will memorize together one verse each session. Encourage youth to select a partner to whom they can be accountable and with whom they can recite memory verses.

Display in jumbled order the words of 1 John 1:5. Challenge the youth to arrange the words in correct order, referring to their Bibles if necessary. When they have the words in correct order, lead the group to recite the verse in unison. Remove two cards and challenge youth to recite the verse filling in the missing words. Remove two more words and recite again. Repeat the card removal until youth say the verse by memory. Challenge them to memorize John 4:24 and 1 John 4:8 at home. (OPTION: If your group is large, form three groups and assign one verse to each group to memorize.)

3. Answer Questions About God's Love

• Direct attention to the questions that are hanging from the ceiling. Emphasize that believers have struggled with these questions for centuries. Assign questions to pairs. Suggest that youth scan the topic entitled "God Is Love" for ideas on how to respond to these questions.

4. Examine Fish Symbol

• Explain that the clearest image of God is Jesus Himself. Place a long piece of string in a half circle. Challenge a volunteer to take a second piece of equal length and complete the symbol you have begun. The correct answer is to make a fish shape. Direct youth to turn to the beginning of chapter 2 as you explain that the fish symbol was used by early Christians to identify one another during times of persecution. It was a secret sign of the faith. Ask: What do the letters in the Greek word *fish* stand for? (I = Jesus; X = Christ, θ = God; Y = Son, E = Savior).

• Give each youth a credit card sized piece of paper and direct them to write the sign of the fish with the letters and to decorate it. Encourage them to carry it in their wallets.

5. Spell Out Meaning of Incarnation

• Give each youth one of the letters of the word *incarnation*. Challenge them to find a word or phrase in chapter 2 that explains God in human form. For example: "<u>A</u>ll of God" could be used for <u>A</u> and "huma<u>N</u> birth" could be used for <u>N</u>. Direct them to write the words on the letters and tape them in order to the wall. Notice the insight in each word or phrase. Supplement with others you found. Suggest they record the words and phrases in TruthSearch 8 if they have not already done so.

6. Illustrate Human/Divine Concept

• Form two teams. Stretch a rope between the teams. Instruct the "human" team to drop the rope. Ask, What do we lose if Jesus was not human? Then instruct the human team to pick up the rope and the divine team to drop it. Ask, What do we lose if Jesus was not divine? After several have responded, fill in details from chapter 2 and emphasize that Jesus was fully human and fully divine.

7. Write Letters to God

• Provide paper and pencils. Direct youth to write a letter to God as suggested in "Honestly Now" at the end of chapter 1.

• Assign chapters 3 and 4 for the next session. Encourage the youth to complete the TruthSearch activities in each chapter.

The Person I Want to Be

(Chapters 3 and 4)

Background Scripture: Psalm 8:5-6; John 14-16; Romans 7:22-23; Colossians 3

Learning Goals: Youth will understand the role of the Holy Spirit and how He can enable them to carry out God's will for their lives.

AGENDA
1. Talk About Real Things (10 Min.)
2. Explain Trinity (5)
3. Write Job Description (10)
4. Memorize Truths (5)
5. Dream About God's Plans (10)
6. Debate Nature of People (10)
7. Pinpoint New-Life Characteristics (10)

Before the Session

☐ Study chapters 3 and 4 in *Truths That Make a Difference* and complete the TruthSearch activities.

☐ Bring paper and pencils.

☐ Record on small slips of paper the words *PRO* and *CON*. Prepare enough slips for each youth to have one. Have an equal number of each word. Put the slips in a large envelope. Also record this statement on a large strip of paper: PEOPLE ARE BASICALLY BAD.

During the Session

1. Talk About Real Things

• Ask youth to think of things they know are real but that they cannot see, taste, or touch. Ask, How do you know they are real? Explain that we cannot see, taste, or touch the Holy Spirit, but we know He is real because we have experienced His power in our lives.

2. Explain Trinity

• Ask volunteers to define the Trinity. After responses, ask the youth to indicate which illustration of the Trinity in TruthSearch 13 is most helpful and why.

3. Write Job Description

• Arrange pairs. Give each pair a piece of paper and a pencil. Direct them to write a job description for the Holy Spirit. Encourage them to scan John 14-16 and also use as resources the Bible references listed in the subtopics in chapter 3 entitled "A Peek at a Person." and "Now a Word from Jesus." Call for reports.

• Have the youth complete TruthSearch 15. Ask for volunteers to share answers. Ask the youth to share a time they have seen or experienced the Holy Spirit as truth giver ("Spirit of Truth"), teacher, witness, cross-examiner, or living presence. After responses, continue the discussion with such questions as: What would you most like the Holy Spirit to do for you? (See summary list under "Tying Up Loose Ends."

4. Memorize Truths

• Using TruthSearch 23, lead the youth to memorize Psalm 8:5-6.

5. Dream About God's Plans

• Emphasize that living for Christ is more than giving up the "don'ts." Then refer to TruthSearch 20. Instruct youth to dream about all the good plans God has for them. After time for dreaming, encourage each youth to name one good thing they think God has in mind for their future.

• Refer to TruthSearch 24. Ask for a volunteer to explain the meaning of being made in the image of God. After responses, fill in details.

6. Debate Nature of People

• Display the debate statement: PEOPLE ARE BASICALLY BAD. Assign PRO and CON positions by letting youth draw a slip from the envelope. Inform the youth that they are to argue for or against the statement based on what word they drew. Group them according to what they drew. Suggest that they refer to the subtopic in chapter 4 entitled "Are People Essentially Good or Evil?"

Conduct the debate. Close the debate by highlighting significant insights that were presented.

7. Pinpoint New-Life Characteristics

• Direct youth to complete TruthSearch 25. When they are finished, form small groups for them to share their answers. Call for volunteers to share a new-life characteristic they would like to substitute for a basement, old-life characteristic. Emphasize that only in the power of the Holy Spirit can we keep our basement person under control and live according to the new-life characteristics discussed in Colossians 3.

• Assign chapters 5 and 6 for the next session. Encourage the youth to complete the TruthSearch activities in each chapter.

SESSION 3

The Guide for Living
(Chapters 5 and 6)

Background Scripture: John 3:5-6; 2 Timothy 3:16

Learning Goals: Youth will understand that becoming a Christian is the first step to a life worth living and will realize that, because the Bible is God's Word, it is our guide for living.

AGENDA
1. Describe Salvation and Conversion (10 Min.)
2. Write Poems (10)
3. Share Testimonies (10)
4. List Some Facts (10)
5. Memorize Truths (10)
6. Discuss Spiritual Feeding (10)

Before the Session
☐ Study chapters 5 and 6 in *Truths That Make a Difference* and complete the TruthSearch activities.
☐ Enlist youth to give testimonies.
☐ Arrange a display of Bible study resources such as a Bible dictionary, study Bible *(DiscipleYouth Bible)*, commentary, and concordance.
☐ Record on large strips of paper phrases that make up 2 Timothy 3:16.
☐ Ask two youth to be prepared to read John 20:31 and 1 Peter 2:2.

During the Session
1. Describe Salvation and Conversion
• As youth arrive, direct them to describe "salvation" and "conversion" by completing TruthSearch 27. Call for volunteers to share their ideas. Fill in details from the study material.
• Read John 3:3-7. Ask: Why is conversion necessary? Why did Jesus have to die? As youth respond, fill in details from the study material. Assure youth that these questions are difficult to answer.

2. Write Poems

• Guide youth to write a poem about Jesus' sacrifice for them, using the outline in TruthSearch 29. Have volunteers share poems. Sample poem:

JESUS DIED FOR ME

GAVE HURT

EXCRUCIATING WILLING DEDICATED

CARED DEEPLY FOR ME

LOVE

3. Share Testimonies

• Arrange for several Christian youth to share a sixty-second testimony about their conversion experience. Note ways the testimonies were different. Emphasize that God deals individually with each person.

• Invite youth who are not Christians to make that decision. Direct all persons to bow their heads and talk with God. Suggest that youth who want to make a decision see you after class or telephone you.

4. List Some Facts

• Point out that the best way to live our conversion is to study the Bible to discover what Jesus wants us to do. Ask, Why is the Bible so valuable? (Refer to TruthSearch 33 during this discussion.)

• Ask youth to complete TruthSearch 34. Share answers.

5. Memorize Truths

• Guide the youth in memorizing 2 Timothy 3:16 by giving several youth a strip that contains a word or phrase from the verse. Arrange the youth in order and direct them to say their verse portion in order. Cue one youth to sit down and challenge the others to repeat his or her part. Have several more sit down in turn. Call for volunteers to recite the entire verse.

• Direct attention to the display of Bible study resources. Briefly explain the purpose of each resource.

• Ask for volunteers to define these terms from 2 Timothy 3:16: *inspired, profitable, reproof, correction, training in righteousness*. Have them look up the terms in a Bible dictionary and read the verse from several different translations to clarify the meaning of each term.

• Refer the youth to the matching activity in TruthSearch 35. Call for volunteers to give answers.

6. Discuss Spiritual Feeding

• Call on the youth enlisted to read John 20:31 and 1 Peter 2:2. State that the main purposes of the Bible are to bring persons to faith in Jesus and to help believers grow in their faith. Challenge youth to fill in the spoons in TruthSearch 36. Encourage volunteers to share what they wrote in one spoon.

• Assign chapters 7 and 8 for the next session.

The Relationships That Count
(Chapters 7 and 8)

Background Scripture: 1 Thessalonians 5:16-18; Acts 2:42

Learning Goals: Youth will discover specific actions that can help develop and improve their relationships with God and fellow believers.

AGENDA
1. Discuss Attitudes About Prayer (15 Min.)
2. Examine Model Prayer (15)
3. Memorize Truths (10)
4. Affirm Serving Abilities (10)
5. Compose Group Prayer (10)

Before the Session
☐ Study chapters 7 and 8 in *Truths That Make a Difference* and complete the TruthSearch activities.
☐ On four large strips of poster board (different colors) print the following words: *AGREE, DISAGREE, STRONGLY AGREE, STRONGLY DISAGREE*.
☐ Bring paper and markers.

During the Session
1. Discuss Attitudes About Prayer
  • Direct attention to the signs on the walls: AGREE, DISAGREE, STRONGLY AGREE, STRONGLY DISAGREE. Read the following statements, one at a time, and ask youth to move to the sign that tells what they think about the statement. For each statement, ask at least one youth to tell why they chose that sign. As you discuss each statement, add information from the sections in chapter 7 listed in parentheses.
  • Prayer is listening to God ("What Is Prayer?").
  • I talk to God with holy language, such as Thee and Thou, rather than everyday language ("What Is Prayer?").

- Prayer doesn't change anything ("Does Prayer Make a Difference?").
- If I pray it will happen ("Does Prayer Make a Difference?").
- Long prayers are better than short ones ("Where Do I Begin?").
- You should pray whether you feel like it or not ("When I Don't Feel Like Praying").

• Reassemble the group and call for a volunteer to read 1 Thessalonians 5:17. Ask: How can we pray without ceasing?

• Form pairs. Direct each pair to complete TruthSearch 39. Ask at least one pair to report on each situation.

2. Examine Model Prayer

• Ask: How is praying like nurturing a friendship? What brings friends closer? Which actions would also help one grow closer to God? (As youth respond, refer to TruthSearch 41.)

• Ask youth to turn in their Bibles to Matthew 6:9-13. Note that this Model Prayer includes most of the things we struggle with and worry about. Direct attention to the statements in TruthSearch 42. Instruct youth to write a phrase from the Model Prayer that relates to each need.

3. Memorize Truths

• Explain that one way to keep our prayer lives vibrant is to spend time with other believers. Use TruthSearch 45 to guide youth in memorizing this verse.

• Ask: What is the purpose of the church? What does Matthew 28:18-20 and Acts 2:42 indicate the church is supposed to do? (List responses on the chalkboard.) How can each individual help the church fulfill its purpose? As these questions are discussed, fill in details from the sections in chapter 8 entitled "What Is the Church" and "Where Is the Church on Monday?"

4. Affirm Serving Abilities

• Direct the youth to begin working on TruthSearch 48. After they have listed several ways they could help carry out the purposes of the church, form groups of three persons. Instruct them to help each other add more actions.

5. Compose Group Prayer

• Lead the youth in a "round robin" prayer using the three elements discussed in "Where Do I Begin?" in chapter 7. Begin by reading Philippians 4:4-7 and instruct youth to take turns around the circle telling God something they are thankful for that no one else has yet stated. The second round, read Mark 11:22-25 and instruct youth to ask God for help with something specific. The third round, read James 5:13-16 and instruct youth to call the name and a need of a particular person. If the need is private, youth can omit the name. Close the prayer.

• Assign chapters 9 and 10 for the next session.

The Symbols and the Hope
(Chapters 9 and 10)

Background Scripture: Romans 6:4; 1 Corinthians 11:23-26; John 14:3

Learning Goals: Youth will discover why Christians celebrate baptism and the Lord's Supper. Youth will claim the assurance that Jesus' return gives to daily living.

AGENDA
1. Play Ordinance Tic-Tac-Toe (20 Min.)
2. Memorize Truths (10)
3. Share Ideas About Future (10)
4. Determine Heaven and Hell Characteristics (10)
5. Celebrate Certainty of Jesus' Second Coming (10)

Before the Session
☐ Study chapters 9 and 10 in *Truths That Make a Difference* and complete the TruthSearch activities in each chapter.
☐ Use heavy paper to make *X* and *O* signs for the tic-tac-toe activity. Record the rules for the game on a large sheet of paper.
☐ Arrange chairs in three rows for the tic-tac-toe activity.
☐ Select a Bible memory method.
☐ Bring writing paper, masking tape, large paper, and pencils.

During the Session
1. Play Ordinance Tic-Tac-Toe
   • Direct attention to the three rows of three chairs placed in the center of the room. Explain that youth will play tic-tac-toe to learn key points about the church ordinances of baptism and the Lord's Supper. Form two teams. Give one team the *X* signs and the other team the *O* signs. Direct them to tape the letter to their chests, open their study books to chapter 9, and have their Bibles in hand. Display the following rules and explain them.

A. The *X* team begins. A teammate chooses the chair of choice and sits in that chair. The team may help select the chair.

B. The teammate may use the study book or a Bible to answer a question but may not receive help from teammates.

C. If teammate answers correctly, person stays in the chair. If not, other team sends representative to answer same question.

D. Each question has a printed sample answer. If you disagree, you can challenge answer by showing answer in the study book or in the Bible.

E. Members of the teams continue taking turns until all youth have had a turn or until all questions have been answered.

F. The first team to seat three in a row wins a round.

The questions:

1. On what item of furniture are the words "In Remembrance of Me" inscribed? *(the Lord's Supper table)*

2. What is a watertight tank large enough for complete immersion in water? *(baptistry)*

3. What is an ordinance? *(decree or command from Christ)*

4. What are the two ordinances observed by Baptists? *(baptism and the Lord's Supper)*

5. True or false: Baptism is necessary for salvation. *(false)*

6. Who baptized Jesus? *(John the Baptist)*

7. Baptism pictures three actions. Name them. *(death, burial, resurrection)*

8. Baptism is an outward symbol of _____ . *(an inward experience or salvation)*

9. One reason Baptists insist on immersion as the method of baptism is that the Greek word for "baptize" means _____ . *(dip, plunge, submerge, or immerse)*

10. True or False: Descriptions of New Testament baptisms suggest that immersion was the method used. *(true)*

11. The third reason Baptists insist on immersion is that baptism is meant to symbolize _____ , _____ , and _____ . *(death, burial, resurrection)*

12. True or false: Baptists believe that babies should be baptized. *(false)*

13. True or false: Baptists believe that all children should be baptized when they reach the age of twelve. *(false)*

14. True or false: Baptists believe that a person should be baptized after he or she believes in Christ. *(true)*

15. True or false: Some Baptist churches request rebaptism when an already baptized believer joins their church. *(true)*

16. Who started the Lord's Supper observance? *(Jesus)*

17. The Lord's Supper is a church _____ . *(ordinance)*

18. Which of these views of the Lord's Supper do Baptists believe: (a) the bread and wine physically become Jesus' body and blood; (b) the bread and wine spiritually become Jesus' body and blood; (c) the bread and wine symbolize Jesus' body and blood. *(statement c)*

19. According to 1 Corinthians 11:24, what does the bread in the Lord's Supper symbolize? *(Jesus' body)*

20. According to 1 Corinthians 11:25, what does the cup in the Lord's Supper symbolize? *(Jesus' blood)*

2. Memorize Truths

• Guide youth to memorize Romans 6:4 using the method youth have enjoyed most in the first four sessions.

3. Share Ideas About Future

• Give each youth a piece of paper and a pencil. Direct them to fold the paper in thirds and then write their forecast of what the world will be like five, ten, and one hundred years from today. Call for volunteers to share what they wrote. Explain that, of course, only Jesus knows our future so listening to Him is the best way to face the future.

• Challenge youth to search "First Things About the Second Coming" in chapter 10 to find at lest five terms that describe the second coming *(examples: certain, unknown date, sudden, mysterious, unexpected)*. After youth have named the terms, ask, How should we prepare for the second coming? *(examples: live faithfully; don't be weary in well-doing—2 Thess. 3:10-13)*.

4. Determine Heaven and Hell Characteristics

• Form two teams. Direct both teams to search "Are Heaven and Hell Real Places?" Ask one team to look for characteristics of hell. Instruct the other team to look for characterisitcs of heaven. Allow three minutes. Challenge youth to race against the clock and against each other by trying to come up with a list longer than the other team.

Call for reports. Ask, What is the way to be certain of your choice? *(choose Jesus for heaven; reject Him for hell)*. Emphasize that we decide where we will go (refer to 2 Pet. 3:9 and TruthSearch 61).

5. Celebrate Certainty of Jesus' second Coming

• Close with an air of celebration, focusing on the second coming of Jesus. Call on each youth in turn to share what they look forward to most about Jesus' second coming (ask them to share what they wrote in Truth-Search 60).

• Lead the youth in a prayer of celebration. Encourage each person to express a statement of thankfulness and expectation about Jesus' second coming. Suggest they state it with enthusiasm as a cheer.

CHRISTIAN GROWTH STUDY PLAN

Preparing Christians to Serve

In the **Christian Growth Study Plan (formerly Church Study Course),** this book *Truths That a Difference* is a resource for course credit in the subject area "Baptist Doctrine" of the Christian Growth category of diploma plans. To receive credit, read the book, complete the learning activities, show your work to your pastor, a staff member or church leader, then complete the information on the next page. The form may be duplicated. Send the completed page to:

Christian Growth Study Plan
127 Ninth Avenue North
MSN 117
Nashville, TN 37234-0117
FAX: 615-251-5067

For information about the Christian Growth Study Plan, refer to the current Christian Growth Study Plan Catalog. Your church office may have a copy. If not, request a free copy from the Christian Growth Study Plan office (615-251-2525).

COURSE NUMBER: CG-0216

PARTICIPANT INFORMATION

Social Security Number	Personal CGSP Number*		Date of Birth

Name (First, MI, Last)

☐Mr. ☐Miss
☐Mrs. ☐

Address (Street, Route, or P.O. Box) | City, State | Home Phone | Zip Code

CHURCH INFORMATION

Church Name

Address (Street, Route, or P.O. Box) | City, State | Zip Code

CHANGE REQUEST ONLY

☐Former Name

☐Former Address | City, State | Zip Code

☐Former Church | City, State | Zip Code

Signature of Pastor, Conference Leader, or Other Church Leader | Date

*New participants are requested but not required to give SS# and date of birth. Existing participants, please give CGSP# when using SS# for the first time. Thereafter, only one ID# is required. *Mail To:* Christian Growth Study Plan, 127 Ninth Ave. North, MSN 117, Nashville, TN 37234-0117. Fax: (615)251-5067